CAMBRIDGE LIBRARY COLLECTION

Books of enduring scholarly value

Cambridge

The city of Cambridge received its royal charter in 1201, having already been home to Britons, Romans and Anglo-Saxons for many centuries. Cambridge University was founded soon afterwards and celebrates its octocentenary in 2009. This series explores the history and influence of Cambridge as a centre of science, learning, and discovery, its contributions to national and global politics and culture, and its inevitable controversies and scandals.

A History of the Cambridge University Press 1521–1921

Published to mark the four hundredth anniversary of the first book to be printed in Cambridge by John Siberch in 1521, this book traces the development of the Press over four centuries. S. C. Roberts, who became Secretary to the Press Syndicate in 1922, blends archival research with an anecdotal style to produce this informative account. Appendices list the university printers up to 1921, including most famously Thomas Thomas, John Legate, Thomas Buck and John Baskerville, and the books published in each year between 1521 and 1750 by authors such as Erasmus, George Herbert, John Donne, John Milton, Isaac Newton and Thomas Browne. Aimed at the general reader, this lively account of the Press's major achievements is illustrated with a number of portraits and historical documents and remains a useful introduction to the history of the oldest publishing house in the world.

T0373816

Cambridge University Press has long been a pioneer in the reissuing of out-of-print titles from its own backlist, producing digital reprints of books that are still sought after by scholars and students but could not be reprinted economically using traditional technology. The Cambridge Library Collection extends this activity to a wider range of books which are still of importance to researchers and professionals, either for the source material they contain, or as landmarks in the history of their academic discipline.

Drawing from the world-renowned collections in the Cambridge University Library, and guided by the advice of experts in each subject area, Cambridge University Press is using state-of-the-art scanning machines in its own Printing House to capture the content of each book selected for inclusion. The files are processed to give a consistently clear, crisp image, and the books finished to the high quality standard for which the Press is recognised around the world. The latest print-on-demand technology ensures that the books will remain available indefinitely, and that orders for single or multiple copies can quickly be supplied.

The Cambridge Library Collection will bring back to life books of enduring scholarly value across a wide range of disciplines in the humanities and social sciences and in science and technology.

A History of the Cambridge University Press 1521–1921

SYDNEY CASTLE ROBERTS

CAMBRIDGE
UNIVERSITY PRESS

CAMBRIDGE UNIVERSITY PRESS

Cambridge New York Melbourne Madrid Cape Town Singapore São Paolo Delhi

Published in the United States of America by Cambridge University Press, New York

www.cambridge.org
Information on this title: www.cambridge.org/9781108002516

This edition first published 1921
This digitally printed version 2009

ISBN 978-1-108-00251-6

A HISTORY OF THE
CAMBRIDGE UNIVERSITY PRESS
1521–1921

CAMBRIDGE UNIVERSITY PRESS

C. F. CLAY, Manager

LONDON : FETTER LANE, E.C. 4

NEW YORK : THE MACMILLAN CO.
BOMBAY ⎫
CALCUTTA ⎬ MACMILLAN AND CO., Ltd.
MADRAS ⎭
TORONTO : THE MACMILLAN CO. OF
CANADA, Ltd.
TOKYO : MARUZEN-KABUSHIKI-KAISHA

THE PITT PRESS BUILDING

A HISTORY OF THE CAMBRIDGE UNIVERSITY PRESS

1521–1921

BY

S. C. ROBERTS, M.A.

SOMETIME SCHOLAR OF
PEMBROKE COLLEGE

CAMBRIDGE
AT THE UNIVERSITY PRESS

1921

PREFACE

A S may be inferred from the title-page, this book has been written to mark the four hundredth anniversary of Cambridge printing.

Of the original authorities used in its compilation the most valuable has been the large collection of documents relating to the Press which are preserved in the Registry of the University. Access to this collection has enabled me to glean some fresh information concerning the careers of the university printers and a series of accounts and vouchers from 1697 to 1742 has brought to light several new titles of books printed at Cambridge during that period.

The making of this book, however, would not have been feasible, in the limited time at my disposal, had I not been free to use the work of the pioneers, from Christopher Wordsworth and Henry Bradshaw onwards, and the chief items of this work are recorded in the short bibliography on page xiii.

In addition, my personal obligations are many: Mr Francis Jenkinson, University Librarian, Mr Charles Sayle, Mr A. T. Bartholomew, and many other members of the Library staff have helped me ungrudgingly, both in putting their own special knowledge at my command and in guiding me to the proper authorities; the Registrary (Dr J. N. Keynes) and his staff have similarly given me ready access to the documents in their charge; Mr J. B. Peace, University Printer, provided me with the picture which serves as frontispiece and with the revised plan of the Press buildings; Mr G. J. Gray corrected several of my statements in proof and gave me the benefit of his own latest researches into the career of John Siberch before they were published; to many other friends (including my colleagues in the several departments of the Press) I am indebted for items of advice and help too many to be enumerated.

I have also to thank the Master of Trinity College for leave to reproduce the portrait of Bentley; Messrs Bowes and Bowes for the blocks used on pp. 6 and 14; and the Cambridge Antiquarian Society for leave to make use of the papers on Cambridge printing published in their *Proceedings*.

Those who are familiar with the *Catalogue of Cambridge Books* and the *Biographical Notes on Cambridge Printers* will appreciate the measure of my debt to the work of the late Robert Bowes. When, in 1913, I sent him a copy of a magazine article on the University Press, he wrote:

I am by it carried back to my pleasant work of 25 to 30 years ago, and I am very glad in my 78th year to see younger men interesting themselves in the subject.

Time has robbed me of the pleasure of offering him
a work which owes much to his research.

Finally, it should be stated that the book attempts
to trace the general history of Cambridge printing
and not to enter into the finer points of bibliographical technique. Similarly, only the briefest
sketch is given of the growth of Cambridge publishing in the last 50 years; to do more would be
to cross the border-line between history and adver-
tisement. In Appendix II I have carried on the
work begun by Mr Jenkinson for another 100
years. The list of books, though it may claim some
new titles, makes no pretension to finality; it is
rather a starting-point for the professed biblio-
grapher.

                                        S. C. R.

1 *August* 1921.

CONTENTS

ILLUSTRATIONS

BIBLIOGRAPHY

Cole MSS. British Museum.
Minute Books of the Syndics of the Press.
Registry MSS. relating to the Press.
University Press Accounts.

ALDIS, H. G. The Book-Trade, 1557–1625 (*Camb. Hist. of Eng. Lit.* IV). Cambridge, 1909.

ALLEN, P. S. Opus Epistolarum Des. Erasmi. 3 vols. Oxford, 1906–13.

ARBER, E. A Transcript of the Registers of the Company of Stationers of London, 1554–1640. 5 vols. Privately printed, 1875–94.

BARTHOLOMEW, A. T. Catalogue of Cambridge Books bequeathed to the University by J. W. Clark. Cambridge, 1912.

BARTHOLOMEW, A. T. and CLARK, J. W. Richard Bentley, D.D. A Bibliography. Cambridge, 1908.

BOWES, R. Biographical notes on the University printers (*C.A.S. Proc.* V. 283–363). Cambridge, 1886.

Catalogue of Cambridge Books. Cambridge, 1894.

Note on the Cambridge University Press, 1701–1707 (*C.A.S. Proc.* VI. 362). Cambridge, 1891.

On a copy of Linacre's Galen de Temperamentis (*C.A.S. Proc.* IX. 1).

BOWES, R. and GRAY, G. J. John Siberch: bibliographical notes, 1886–1905. Cambridge, 1906.

BRADSHAW, H. Henrici Bulloci Oratio. With bibliographical introduction. Cambridge, 1886.

Cambridge Historical Register to 1910. Ed. J. R. TANNER. Cambridge, 1917.

CARTER, E. History of the University of Cambridge. London, 1753.

COOPER, C. H. Annals of Cambridge. 5 vols. Cambridge, 1842–1908.

COOPER, C. H. Athenae Cantabrigienses. 3 vols. Cambridge, 1858–1913.

CRANAGE, D. H. S. and STOKES, H. P. The Augustinian Friary in Cambridge and the History of its Site (*C.A.S. Proc.* XXII. 53). Cambridge, 1921.

DARLOW, T. H. and MOULE, H. F. Historical Catalogue of the printed editions of Holy Scripture. 4 vols. London, 1903–11.

DUFF, E. G. The English Provincial Printers, Stationers and Bookbinders to 1557. Cambridge, 1912.

DYER, G. Privileges of the University of Cambridge. London, 1824.

GED, W. Biographical Memoirs of. London, 1781, and New-castle, 1819.

Grace Book A. Ed. S. M. LEATHES. Cambridge, 1897.
  B. Parts I, II. Ed. MARY BATESON. Cambridge, 1903, 1905.
  Γ. Ed. W. G. SEARLE. Cambridge, 1908.
  Δ. Ed. J. VENN. Cambridge, 1910.

GRAY, G. J. Bibliography of the works of Sir I. Newton. Ed. 2. Cambridge, 1907.
  Index to the Cole MSS. Cambridge, 1912.
  John Siberch. Cambridge, 1921.
  The earlier Cambridge stationers and bookbinders, and the first Cambridge printer. Oxford, 1904.

GRAY, G. J. and PALMER, W. M. Abstracts from the Wills of Printers, Binders, and Stationers of Cambridge, 1504–1699. London, 1915.

HART, H. Charles, Earl Stanhope and the Oxford University Press (Collectanea III). Oxford, 1896.

HERBERT, W. Typographical antiquities. Begun by Joseph Ames. 3 vols. London, 1785–90.

JENKINSON, F. J. H. On a letter from P. Kaetz to J. Siberch (*C.A.S. Proc.* VII. 188). Cambridge, 1890.
  On a unique fragment of a book printed at Cambridge early in the sixteenth century (*C.A.S. Proc.* VII. 104). Cambridge, 1890.

LOFTIE, W. J. A Century of Bibles. London, 1872.

MONK, J. H. The Life of Richard Bentley, D.D. London, 1830.

MULLINGER, J. B. The University of Cambridge. 3 vols. Cambridge, 1873–1911.

NEWTH, S. On Bible Revision. London, 1881.

NICHOLS, J. Literary Anecdotes of the Eighteenth Century. 6 vols. London, 1812.

POLLARD, A. W. Fine Books. London, 1912.

REED, T. B. A history of the old English letter foundries. London, 1887.

ROBERTS, W. The Earlier History of English Bookselling. London, 1889.

SAYLE, C. E. Early English printed books in the University Library, Cambridge (1475–1640). 4 vols. Cambridge, 1900–7.

STOKES, H. P. Cambridge Stationers, Printers, Bookbinders, &c. Cambridge, 1919.

The Esquire Bedells of the University of Cambridge (*C.A.S. Publications*, 8° Series, XLV). Cambridge, 1911.

STRAUS, R. and DENT, R. K. John Baskerville. London, 1907.

WILLIS, R. and CLARK, J. W. Architectural History of the University of Cambridge. 4 vols. Cambridge, 1886.

WORDSWORTH, C. The Correspondence of Richard Bentley. 2 vols. London, 1842.

Scholae Academicae. Cambridge, 1877.

I

JOHN SIBERCH

EXCURSIONS into the realm of legend have long served as the traditional method of approach of the academic historian to his subject. True, the story of the foundation of the university of Cambridge by "one Cantaber, a Spaniard, about 370 years before Christ," or, as Fisher described him in 1506, "Cantaber, a king of the East Saxons, who had been educated at Athens," is now definitely rejected as unhistorical; but it was only in 1914 that the name of Sigebert, King of the East Angles, was removed from the list of royal benefactors[1].

University printing, like the university itself, has its Apocrypha. Edmund Carter, writing in 1753, includes a short section on *University Printers*:

> Printing had not been long used in *England* before it was brought hither, but by whom it is difficult to ascertain, tho' it may be supposed that *Caxton*, (who is said to be the first that brought this curious art into *England*, and was a *Cambridgeshire* Man, born at *Caxton* in that County, from which he takes his Name) might Erect a Press at *Cambridge*, as well as at *Westminster*, under the care of one of his Servants; (for it is Conjectured, he brought several from *Germany* with him). The first Book we find an Account of, that was Printed here, is a Piece of *Rhetoric*, by one *Gull. de Saona*, a Minorite; Printed at *Cambridge* 1478; given by Archbp. Parker to *Bennet* College Library. It is in Folio, the Pages not Numbered, and without ketch Word, or Signatures.

[1] *Cambridge Historical Register*, pp. 1, 168.

Alas for Carter's pious suppositions! Caxton, according to his own testimony, was born in Kent and Cambridge can claim only to be the place of compilation of the *Rhetorica*; the phrase at the end of the book, *Compilata in Universitate Cantabrigiae*, no doubt led to the entry being made in the catalogue in the form *Rhetorica nova, impressa Cantab, fo.* 1478, and the mistake persisted for two centuries.

Nor is Oxford without a controversial prologue to the story of its printing. In the first Oxford book the date appears in the colophon as MCCCCLXVIII and for long it was sought to establish the claim that Oxford printing preceded Caxton. But though it has been contended that the ground for the claim "has not yet entirely slipped away," it is now generally accepted by bibliographers that the printer omitted an x from the date, which should in fact be MCCCCLXXVIII.

"The oldest of all inter-university sports," said Maitland, "was a lying match."

To return to Cambridge, we are on firmer, though not very spacious, ground, when we come to the name of John Siberch, the first Cambridge printer. "True it is," says Thomas Fuller, "it was a great while before Cambridge could find out the right knack of printing, and therefore they preferred to employ Londoners therein. . . . but one Sibert, University Printer, improved that mystery to good perfection."

Of the life of Siberch, either at Cambridge or elsewhere, we know little. He was the friend of

several great humanists of the period, including
Erasmus; he was in Louvain, evidently, in 1518.
"I was surprised," writes Erasmus to John Cae-
sarius on 5 April of that year, "that John Siberch
came here without your letter."

The earliest appearance of his name on a title-
page is in 1520, when Richard Croke's *Introduc-
tiones in rudimenta Graeca* was printed at Cologne
"expensis providi viri domini Ioannis Laer de Siborch."[1] His full name, then (of which there are
many forms), is John Lair and his place of origin
Siegburg, a small town south-west of Cologne.

A discovery made by Mr Gordon Duff in the
Westminster Abbey Library in 1889 makes it almost certain that Siberch was already in England
when Croke's book was printed; for in a copy of
a book bound by Siberch there was found, besides
two printed fragments and a letter from Petrus
Kaetz[2], a portion of the manuscript of the *Rudimenta Graeca*. It seems clear, therefore, that Siberch
was in England when proofs and 'copy' of the work
were sent to him.

Richard Croke (afterwards the first Public Orator) was at this time the enthusiastic leader of Greek
studies in Cambridge. He had earned fame as a
teacher at Cologne, Louvain, Leipzig, and Dresden
and, in succession to his friend Erasmus, was
appointed Reader in Greek to the university in
1519. His text-book could not be printed in
England, because there was as yet no Greek fount

---

1 The binding of a copy of this book in Lincoln Cathedral is
almost certainly the work of Siberch.   2 See below, p. 14.

owned by an English printer; and it is quite probable, as Mr Duff suggests, that John Siberch,
himself settled in Cambridge, had undertaken to
have Croke's work printed by a friend, possibly by
his old master, in Cologne. Possibly, too, Croke
may have previously met Siberch in Germany and,
with Erasmus, have been responsible for his coming
to Cambridge. This, of course, is conjectural, but
of the friendship between Erasmus and Siberch
there is no doubt, since, in a letter from Erasmus
to Dr Robert Aldrich, written on Christmas Day
1525, there is a message sent to "veteres sodales
Phaunum, Omfridum, Vachanum, Gerardum, et
Joannem Siburgum, bibliopolas."

From this it would naturally be inferred that
Siberch was still in Cambridge in 1525, but his name
does not appear in the Subsidy Roll of 1523–24 and
it is probable, therefore, that, unknown to Erasmus,
he left in the early part of 1523[1].

Siberch, then, probably lived in Cambridge from
1520 to 1523, a period during which the labours
of the first Cambridge humanists were beginning to
bear fruit. In 1497, the Lady Margaret, mother
of Henry VII, had appointed as her confessor John
Fisher, Master of Michaelhouse; and "to the wealth
and liberality of the one," in Mullinger's words,
"and the enlightened zeal and liberality of the other
the university is chiefly indebted for that new life
and prosperity which soon after began to be per-
ceptible in its history."

To the Lady Margaret were due the foundation

---

[1] See G. J. Gray, *John Siberch* (1921).

of St John's and Christ's Colleges and the Professorship and Preachership which bear her name; Fisher,
afterwards Bishop of Rochester and President of
Queens' College, was the first holder of the Divinity
chair and it was at his invitation that Erasmus, who
had taken a degree in divinity in Cambridge in
1506, came to live, in 1509 or 1510, in the turret-
chamber of Queens'. Though it is, perhaps, as the
first teacher of Greek (himself for the most part
self-taught and not, as Gibbon says, the importer of
Greek from Oxford) that Erasmus is most famous,
the result of his first lectures was disappointing:

So far I have lectured on the grammar of Chrysoloras,
but to few hearers; perhaps I shall have a larger
audience when I begin the grammar of Theodorus,
perhaps I shall take up a theological lectureship.

This last hope was fulfilled in 1511, when Erasmus was elected to the Lady Margaret's professorship of divinity. His letters are full of petulant
complaints which may be taken as seriously as
those of Gray in later years. He sees no hope of
lecture-fees since his conscience will not let him
rob 'naked men,' and only by touting does it appear possible to get pupils. The college beer is bad
and the townsmen boorish. So he retires to his
garret in Queens' and applies himself to his work
on the New Testament (*Novum Instrumentum*) and
his edition of St Jerome, both of which were to
play an important part in preparing the way for
the Reformation in England.

When weary of study, "for lacke of better exercise he would take his horse and ryde about the

Market Hill." But he has words of praise for the Cambridge school of theology:

In the University of Cambridge instead of sophistical arguments, their theologians debate in a sober, sensible manner and depart wiser and better men.

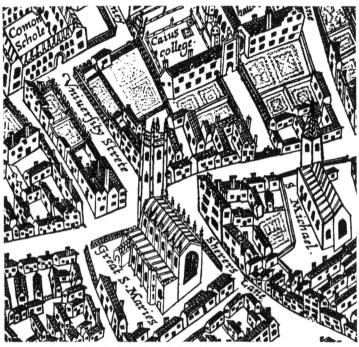

PART OF HAMOND'S PLAN OF CAMBRIDGE, 1592
(*showing Siberch's house*)

It was to this Cambridge and, probably, to this patron in Cambridge that John Siberch came. The single reference to his place of residence and to his position in the university occurs in the *Annals* of Dr Caius:

The space (he writes) between the gate of humility and the gate of Virtue was formerly occupied by a tenement called the King's Arms. This was once the residence of John Sibert, alias Siberch, the University Printer, who printed some books of John Lydgate and others, and of Erasmus when he was residing at Cambridge.

The "tenement called the King's Arms" explains the use by Siberch of the royal arms as a printer's device; but although *cum gratia et privilegio* appears on the title-page of several books printed by him, there is no official confirmation of his having held the office of university printer[1].

There are entries, however, in *Grace Books* and in the *Audit Book* of the university which show that in 1520 or 1521 the university advanced to him the sum of twenty pounds:

Obligatur doctor Manfeld loco et vice magistri Norres pro summa pecunie quam recepit Johannes bibliopola ab universitate[2].

Probably, Mr Duff suggests, this sum of money—a larger amount than a university stationer's fee—may have been advanced with a view to helping Siberch in the establishment of a press.

The debt is entered in the proctors' accounts until the year 1524–25 and in *Grace Book B* it is recorded under the date 1538–9 that John Law, an alien priest, with Drs Ridley, Bulloke, Wakefield, and Maundefelde owed £20 sterling to the university, for which they had given a bond with their signature and seals; reference is made to

[1] John Tabor, Registrary from 1600 to 1645, wrote in 1620: "John Seberch a printer of the University of Cambridge was the first that printed in England in greeke letter" (Registry MS 33. 2. 17).
[2] *Grace Book* Γ, p. 196.

this bond in the *Audit Book* under the dates 1546, 1549, and 1553. From the description of Siberch as "presbiter alienigena" Mr Duff infers that Siberch eventually forsook printing for the Church.

Such are the fragmentary references that have survived concerning the career of the first Cambridge printer.

Fortunately, however, eight complete specimens of his book-printing have been preserved:

1 The first Cambridge book (of which a page is shown in facsimile) reflects the atmosphere of the time. It is the *Oratio* delivered by Henry Bullock, D.D., Fellow of Queens' College and afterwards Vice-Chancellor, in honour of the visit of Cardinal Wolsey to the university in the autumn of 1520. The 'frequentissimus cetus' before whom the oration was given included the imperial ambassadors and several bishops.

The cardinal was lodged at Queens' College and both town and university delighted to honour him, as may be seen from the following items from the proctors' accounts:

To the Vicechancellor for expences in going round the town with the mayor, to cleanse the streets against the coming of the Cardinal, 2s 2d.

Gifts to the Cardinal: for wine £3 6s 8d; for carrying the same to Queens coll. 12d; for 2 oxen, £3 7s 8d; for 6 swans, 28s 8d; for 6 great pikes, 33s 4d; for 6 shell fish, 4s 4d; for a river fish called a breme, 6s 8d.

For repairing the streets on the Cardinal's coming, 13d.

To 2 scholars who carried an altar on the coming of the Cardinal, 4d.

DOCTISSIMI VIRI HENRICI

Bulloci theologiæ doctoris oratio, habita Cantabri
giæ, in frequentissimo cetu, præsentibus Cæsaris ora
toribus, & nonnullis alijs episcopis, ad reuerendiss.
D. Thomam Cardinalem titulo sanctæ Ce=
ciliæ, Legatū a latere, Archiepiscopū
Eboracensem, & Angliæ su=
premum Cancelarium.

 O N expectabis multo omnium fæliciss̄i
N me Cardinalis, quod hac breui oratiun=
cula, immensam illam laudum tuarum are
am uelimus ingredi, uel tantulo uerborum numero
uir utum tuarum omnium summam perstringere,
quando eas uix ingenti uolumine, tantum abest, ut
sermone non dico diurno, sed ne semestri quidem
aut annuo uel connumerare quispiā possit. Nos uer
ba facturi sumus de hisce duntaxat rebus perpaucis
illis quidem, sed quæ ob earundē magnitudinem ĕṣ=
sent omnibus, nedū adstantibus, cognita (quod hos
meos spiritus non mediocriter recreat) uiderent for=
tassis incredibilia, nec citra assentationis notam referri
posse, cæterū tantū aberit hic noster sermo ab assen=
tatione, quātum abest a necessitate. Quippe huiusce
modi sunt proceres humanissimi, huius amplissimi
Præsulis

The style of the oration is even more lavish than the ceremonial preparations. "Scarcely from the obsequious senates of Tiberius and Domitian did the incense of flattery rise in denser volume or in coarser fumes."[1]

Bradshaw pointed out that the type used for the printing of the *Oratio* appears to be quite new. Many of the lines are wavy and irregular and there are no woodcut initials or ornaments of any kind. The second imprint, at the end of the book, runs: *Impressa est haec oratiūcula Cantabrigiae, per me Ioannem Siberch, post natum saluatorem, Millesimo quingentesimo uicesimoprimo. Mense Februario.* A second impression was printed a few months later and issued with Siberch's third book.

Four libraries possess copies: the British Museum; the Bodleian Library; Lambeth Palace; and Archbishop Marsh's Library, St Patrick's, Dublin. Cambridge unfortunately has no copy.

11 The second Cambridge book is the rarest of all those printed by Siberch, only one copy (John Selden's, bequeathed to the Bodleian Library in 1659) having been preserved.

It contains a letter addressed by a 'certain faithful Christian' to 'all Christians' and a sermon of Augustine *De miseria ac brevitate vitae*, of which the full title may be read in the facsimile. In addition to its uniqueness, the book has a further interest in that the Greek motto on the title-page was printed from the first genuine moveable Greek type used in England. Woodcuts depicting scenes from the

1 Mullinger, I, 546.

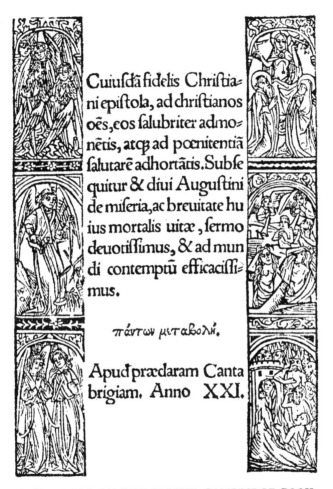

Cuiuſdã fidelis Chriſtia=
ni epiſtola, ad chriſtianos
oẽs, eos ſalubriter admo=
nẽtis, atꝗ ad pœnitentiã
ſalutarẽ adhortãtis. Subſe
quitur & diui Auguſtini
de miſeria, ac breuitate hu
ius mortalis uitæ, ſermo
deuotiſſimus, & ad mun
di contemptũ efficaciſſi=
mus.

πάντων μεταβολή.

Apud prædaram Canta
brigiam. Anno XXI.

TITLE-PAGE OF THE SECOND CAMBRIDGE BOOK

Last Judgment and probably copied from a German *Book of Hours* are also used on the title-page.

III The next book contains Lucian περὶ διψάδων translated by Henry Bullock, together with a re-issue of the *Oratio*. On the title-page there appears for the first time the elaborate border with the Arma Regia (the sign of the house in which Siberch lived) at the foot. No other ornament is used, but Greek type appears on the title-page, in the dedication, and at the end of the book.

Four copies are known: two in the British Museum, one in St John's College, Cambridge, and one at Lambeth Palace.

IV The fourth book, Archbishop Baldwin's *Sermo de altaris sacramento* (1521), contains for the first time a woodcut initial and the Arma Regia in another form. The book is dedicated to Nicholas West, Bishop of Ely, and in the dedication Siberch claims to be the first printer to use Greek type in England—"Ioannes Siberch primus utriusque linguae in Anglia impressor."

Nine copies have survived: two in the Bodleian, two in the University Library, Cambridge, one in Trinity College, Cambridge, one in Magdalene College, Cambridge, one in All Souls' College, Oxford, one in Lincoln and one in Peterborough Cathedral Library[1].

V The next book has many points of interest. In the first place, it is by the printer's friend, Erasmus, and its title gives a brief survey of the manner of its composition: *Libellus de Conscribendis*

[1] The Bury St Edmund's copy is now lost.

*epistolis, Autore D. Erasmo, opus olim ab eodem cœptum, sed prima manu, mox expoliri cœptum, sed intermissum, Nunc primum prodit in lucem....*MDXXI.

Secondly, it is the first book of any size undertaken by Siberch. "Ignosces," he pleads, "candide lector iam primum experienti mihi." Further, the phrase *Cum gratia et privilegio* is now used on the title-page for the first time; for this leave had probably been obtained through Bishop Fisher, in a dedication to whom the printer calls himself 'Cantabrigiensis typographus.'

Four copies are known: two in the British Museum, one in St John's College, Cambridge, and one in Corpus Christi College, Cambridge; the last has an additional interest in that it was bound by Nicholas Speryng.

VI The sixth of the books printed by Siberch is the commonest. It is a translation of Galen by Thomas Linacre: *Caleni Pergamensis de Temperamentis, et de inaequali intemperie libri tres Thoma Linacro Anglo interprete.*

It is described on the title-page, which has the same border-device as III, as "opus non medicis modo, sed et philosophis oppido q*uam* necessariu*m*"; it is dedicated to Pope Leo X and printed "cum gratia et privilegio."

The existing copies of the book are in two states: a copy in the first state was found by the late Mr Robert Bowes in the library of Trinity College, Dublin, containing only the *De Temperamentis* and having on the last leaf but one a woodcut of the Adoration of the Shepherds. The copy in the

ONTIO QVAM AN=
GLICE HABVIT RE=
VERENDVS PATER
IOANNES ROFFEN=
SIS EPISCOPVS IN
celeberrimo Nobilium Con=
uentu Londini, eo die, quo Martini Lutheri fcri=
pta publico apparatu in ignem coniecta funt, uer=
fa in Latinū per Richardum Pacæum a Sereniffi=
mi REGIS ANGLIE Secretis, verum Grece
∴   & Latine Peritiffimum,   ∴

CVM GRATIA ET PRIVILEGIO ∴

TITLE-PAGE OF FISHER'S SERMON

Royal College of Physicians consists of this first issue with the second essay added. The remaining ten copies—University Library, Cambridge (2); Bodleian Library (2); British Museum; Trinity College, Cambridge; All Souls' College, Oxford; Hunterian Museum, Glasgow; the Duke of Devonshire; Mr Bowes—are in the second state, containing both the *De Temperamentis* and the *De inaequali intemperie*, the last two leaves of the former essay as they appear in the first state being cancelled.

VII The full title of the seventh Cambridge book may be read in the facsimile here shown. It is a Latin translation of the sermon delivered in London by Fisher when Luther's books were publicly burned.

Siberch has now discarded his ornamental title-border, but at the end of the book there appears a new device, embodying his trade-mark and initials. The book was printed late in 1521 and probably issued early in the January of the next year.

Five copies are known: two in the Bodleian Library; one in the University Library, Cambridge; one in Magdalene College, Cambridge; and one in the John Rylands Library, Manchester.

VIII The last of the eight books printed by Siberch of which complete copies survive is *Papyrii Gemini Eleatis Hermathena, seu De Eloquentiae Victoria*, printed on the 8th December, 1522. There are three different states of the title-page and six complete copies are known: University Library, Cambridge; British Museum; St John's College, Oxford; Archbishop Marsh's Library, St Patrick's, Dublin; Duke of Devonshire; Lincoln Cathedral Library.

To these eight books must be added the *De octo partium orationis constructione libellus* of Lily and Erasmus, two leaves of which were found in the book bound by Siberch which Mr Duff discovered at Westminster. This *libellus*, originally written by William Lily and revised, at Colet's suggestion, by Erasmus, was a popular school book of the period.

It was in the binding of the same book that the letter from Petrus Kaetz, a Dutch printer, was also found. This letter has many points of interest. Kaetz sends Siberch "25 prognostications and 3 New Testaments small," as well as a parcel to be delivered to Niclas [Speryng] and we may fittingly conclude our notice of Siberch with the tribute of a contemporary to his prospects as a printer:

Know, Jan Siborch (writes Petrus Kaetz) that I have received your letter as [well as specimens] of your type, and it is very good; if you can otherwise...and conduct yourself well, then you will get enough to print.
(Translation by Dr Hessels, Jenkinson, *C.A.S.* VIII, 186.)

TRADE-MARK OF JOHN SIBERCH

II

THE CHARTER—THOMAS THOMAS AND THE STATIONERS

THOUGH it may not be clear to what extent John Siberch was officially recognised as printer to the university, it is evident that no successor to him was immediately appointed. University stationers and bookbinders, however, had been for some time established in a privileged position. As early as 1276 we find a reference to the "writers, illuminators, and stationers, who serve the scholars only," and in a note on this phrase Fuller defines the *stationarii* as "publicly avouching the sale of staple-books in standing shops (whence they have their names) as opposite to such circumforanean pedlers (ancestors to our modern Mercuries and hawkers) which secretly vend prohibited books."

In 1350 John Hardy, procurator of the Corpus Christi Gild, is described as "stationarius of the University" and we learn something of the stationers' duties from the prohibition by Convocation in 1408 of the use in schools of "any book or tract compiled by John Wiclif, or any one else in his time or since or to be compiled thereafter" unless first examined by the universities and afterwards approved by the Archbishop. After the book had been finally sanctioned, it was to be delivered "in the name and by the authority of the University to the stationers to be copied; and a faithful collation being made, the original should be deposited in the chest of either University, there to remain for ever."

In his edition of *Grace Book A* (1454–88) Sir Stanley Leathes summarises the position of the *Stationaries* as follows:

They were not students, nor were they exactly servants or tradesmen. They were the official agents of the University for the sale of pledges, and official valuers of manuscripts and other valuables offered as security. They seem to have received an occasional fee from the Chest....Like the servants and tradesmen dependent on the University they were under the University jurisdiction.

Many of the stationers were binders as well and the keeping of the university chest was included in their duties; from the will of Petrus Breynans (*c.* 1504) it also appears that they were provided by the university with a distinctive gown[1].

At the beginning of the sixteenth century, we find the stationers involved in one of the many disputes between university and town, damaging alike to study and to business. In 1502 both parties besought the "amicable interference" of the Lady Margaret, who counselled arbitration; the result was an "indenture of covenant" executed by university and town "pursuant to the award of Sir Thomas Frowycke and the other arbitrators." One clause in the indenture runs:

ITEM, yt ys covenanted, accorded, and agreed bitwene the said Parties, accordinge to the said Award, that all

---

1 See also *Grace Book A*, p. 117, where there is the following item in the proctors' accounts for 1476–7:

Item stacionario pro toga   xiij^s iiij^d

Bedells of the said Universitie, and all Mancipills, Cooks, Butlers, and Launders of everye Colledge, Hostell, and of other places ordeyned for Scolers, Students, and places of religion in the said Universitie, and all appotycares, Stacioners, Lymners, Schryveners, Parchment-makers, Boke-bynders, Phisitions, Surgeons, and Barbers in the sayd Universitie...shall be reputed and taken as Common Ministers and Servants of the said Universitie, as longe as they shall use eny such occupacion, and shall have and enjoye lyke privilege as a Scolers Servant of the same Universitie shall have and enjoye....[1]

In the list at the end of the award containing the names of those privileged by the university, the last entry is "Garreit Stacioner." This "Garreit" is the stationer and binder generally known as Garrett Godfrey. When he first began business in Cambridge is not known, but more than fifty specimens of his binding, dating from 1499 to 1535, have survived. We know also that he was churchwarden of Great St Mary's in 1516 and again in 1521 and that he died in 1539[2].

Erasmus refers to him in 1516 as his "old host, Garrett the bookseller" (which suggests that he stayed in his house during his first visit to Cambridge), and in 1525 sends a message, already quoted, to Garrett and other booksellers.

Another stationer and bookbinder of the period is Nicholas Spierinck (Speryng), whose name first appears in *Grace Book B* under the date 1505–6.

1 Cooper, *Annals*, I, 262.
2 "Garard et spierinck" were sureties for Jerome Leonard, the Carmelite, in 1520–1 (*Grace Book B*, p. 91). In the same volume it is recorded that Garrett Godfrey bound a book for Cardinal Wolsey in 1528–9 (p. 152).

R. 2

Little is known of him as a stationer. He was a Dutchman by birth and, like Garrett Godfrey, was a friend of Erasmus and a churchwarden of Great St Mary's. His will, of which he appointed Thomas Wendy, the royal physician, as supervisor, shows him to have been a man of property, since he bequeathed to Nycholas Spyrynke, his "sonnes sonne," the "howse of the Crosse Keyes"—a brewery in Magdalene Street[1]; of his work as a binder nearly fifty examples remain.

The third of the Cambridge stationers of this period whom we must consider is Segar Nicholson. He also came from Holland, and, as Mr G. J. Gray remarks, affords an early example of a member of the university engaging in business, being a pensioner of Gonville Hall from 1520 to 1523. His career has more varied features than those of his fellow-stationers.

In 1529 he was charged with holding Protestant views and further with the unlawful possession of Luther's books and other heretical works. Now Luther's books had been publicly burnt in Cambridge eight years before and the ceremony had, as we have seen, been the occasion of a notable sermon by Bishop Fisher. About this time, however, there had grown up a small society of members of the university who were sympathetic towards Lutheran doctrine. They met in secret in the White

1 The oak panelling and carved mantelpiece belonging to this ancient house have recently been removed to the new Combination room at Magdalene College (A. B. Gray, *Cambridge revisited*, p. 46).

Horse inn, which stood where are now the back
buildings of the Bull Hotel—a place chosen so
that members might enter unobserved by the back
door and nicknamed 'Germany' by the orthodox[1].
Among the heretics who frequented these meetings
was Segar Nicholson.

Foxe, in his *Acts and Monuments*, gives a sad account of the treatment of Nicholson: "The hand-
ling of this man," he says, "was too too cruel."
After his release from prison, Nicholson remained
a stationer till the age of 60, when he was ordained
deacon by the Bishop of London.

In the meantime the university had taken steps to
ensure the suppression of heretical books. In 1529 a
petition was presented to Cardinal Wolsey, begging:
that for the suppression of error, there should be three
booksellers allowed in Cambridge by the King, who
should be sworn not to bring in or sell any book which
had not first been approved of by the censor of books
in the University, that such booksellers should be men
of reputation and gravity, and foreigners, (so it should
be best for the prizing of books,) and that they might
have the privilege to buy books of foreign merchants[2].

It was, no doubt, as a result of this petition that
five years later Cambridge printing was formally
established by royal charter on 20 July, 1534,
when Henry VIII by letters patent gave licence to
the Chancellor, masters, and scholars
to assign and elect from time to time, by writing under the
seal of the Chancellor of the University, three stationers
and printers, or sellers of books, residing within the

1 See G. F. Browne, *C.A.S. Proc.* III, 407
2 Cooper, *Annals*, I, 329.

University, who might be either aliens or natives, and hold either their own or hired houses. The stationers or printers thus assigned, and every of them, were empowered to print all manner of books approved of by the Chancellor or his vicegerent and three doctors, and to sell and expose to sale in the University or elsewhere within the realm, as well such books as other books printed within or without the realm, and approved of by the Chancellor or his vicegerent and three doctors. If aliens, these stationers or printers were empowered to reside in the University, in order to attend to their business, and were to be reputed and treated as the King's faithful subjects and lieges, and to enjoy the same liberties, customs, laws, and privileges; and to pay and contribute to lot, scot, tax, tallage, and other customs and impositions as the other subjects and lieges of the King. Provided, that the said stationers or printers, being aliens, paid all customs, subsidies, and other monies, for their goods and merchandizes imported or exported, as other aliens[1].

This is the *Magna Carta* of Cambridge printing and Fuller quotes with quiet pride the opinion of Sir Edward Coke that "this University of Cambridge hath power to print within the same 'omnes' and 'omnimodos libros' which the University of Oxford hath not."

We should now expect to see a steady continuance of university printing. But, in spite of the King's letters patent, the history of Cambridge printing for nearly fifty years is a blank. It is true that the university immediately availed itself of

---

[1] Abbreviated translation quoted from Cooper, *Annals*, I, 368. Cooper, however, has "Chancellor *and* his vicegerent *or* three doctors" in one place, and Wordsworth (*Scholae Academicae*, p. 378) copies his mistake.

the privilege conferred upon it, and the "three stationers and printers or sellers of books residing within the university" who were appointed were Nicholas Speryng, Garrett Godfrey, and Segar Nicholson, whose careers have been sketched above. That two of these were bookbinders and churchwardens, that one owned a brewery, and that one took holy orders we have evidence, but of printing there is no trace. The strangest appointment is that of Nicholson, since the aim of the university in petitioning Wolsey for the control of printing and book-selling was the suppression of those Lutheran doctrines for which Nicholson had recently been imprisoned.

But it is clear that, for a time at any rate, the university, while showing no desire to encourage the art of printing, was quick to establish its control and censorship of books.

Some idea of a university bookseller's stock at this time may be obtained from the will of Nicholas Pilgrim[1], appointed in 1539 as successor to Garrett Godfrey, from whom he inherited a "furryd gown and iij presses with a cuttynge knife." Of the 717 books of which an inventory is given in Pilgrim's will 216 were bound and 501 unbound, the whole stock being valued at £26 11s 6d. Most of the books are either editions of the classics or theological works, but there are a few on medical and botanical subjects.

But like Richard Noke, appointed in 1540, and Peter Sheres (1545-6) Pilgrim appears to have been university printer only in name.

1 Gray and Palmer, *Wills of Cambridge Printers*, pp. 10-30.

At the beginning of Elizabeth's reign, when all unlicensed printing was prohibited, the powers of the chancellors of the universities to license books were duly recognised and in 1576, when John Kingston was appointed as printer, the university seems definitely to have contemplated the establishment of a printing-press:

On the 18th of July, Lord Burghley wrote from Theobalds to Dr Goad Vicechancellor and the Heads, with reference to their intention of bringing the exercise of printing into the University, for which purpose they had engaged one Kingston of London, whom they purposed to protect with the University privilege to print Psalters, Books of Common Prayer, and other books in English, for which the Queen had already granted special privileges to William Seres, Richard Jugge, John Day, and others. His Lordship disapproved of any attempts to prejudice the Queen's grants, but thought they might employ an artificer for printing matters pertaining to the schools &c.[1]

In the light of this pronouncement it is easy to understand why John Kingston, who was well-known as a London stationer, printed no books in Cambridge.

At last, in 1583, we come to the name of a university printer who in fact printed books at Cambridge: Thomas Thomas, Fellow of King's College, was appointed University printer by grace of 3 May, 1583, and in the same year began to print a work by William Whitaker.

The Stationers' Company of London quickly seized his press and declared that his attempt was

---

[1] MS Baker XXIX, 374, quoted in Cooper, *Annals*, II, 357.

an infringement of their rights. In a letter to
Burghley, dated 1 June, 1583, the Bishop of
London wrote:

There was alsoe found one presse and furniture which
is saide to belonge to one Thomas a man (as I heare)
utterlie ignoraunte in printinge, and pretendinge that
he entendeth to be the printer for the universitie of
Cambridge.

The Vice-Chancellor and Heads, however, took
up the cause of their printer and in reply to a letter
from Burghley suggesting a conference with the
Stationers, wrote as follows:

Our most humble duties to your honour remembred.
Whereas we understand by your honours letters, that
certain of the company of the stationers in London have
sought to hinder the erecting of a print within the
university of Cambridg, and to impugne that antient
privilege, granted and confirmed by divers princes for
that purpose, to the great benefit of the university and
augmentation of learning: these are in most humble
manner to desire your honour, not so much in respect of
Mr Thomas, who hath already received great injury and
dammage at their hands, as in behalf of the university;
which findeth itself very much aggrieved with the
wrongful detaining of those goods, wherewithal, as we
are persuaded, in right and equity they ought not to
meddle, to continue our honorable patron, and to direct
your favourable warrants to the warden of the stationers,
that he may have his press delivered with speed; lest
that by their means, as he hath been disappointed of
Mr Whitakers book, so by their delays he be prevented
of other books made within the university, and now ready
for the press.

As for the doubts which they caused, rather in respect
of their private gain and commodity, and to bring the
universities more antient privileges in this behalf than

theirs under their jurisdiction at London, than for any other good consideration, the deciding or peril whereof also pertaineth not to them; we dare undertake, in the behalf of Mr Thomas whom we know to be a very godly and honest man, that the press shall not be abused, either in publishing things prohibited, or otherwise inconvenient for the church and state of this realm. And this we promise the rather, for that his grace (whereof we have sent a copy to your honour by himself) was granted unto him upon condition that he should stand bound from time to time to such articles as your honour and the greatest part of the heads of colleges should ty him unto.

And for the conference, whereunto your honour moveth us, if it shall be your honours pleasure, wee, as desirous of peace and concord, (the premisses considered,) shall be ready to shew our willingness thereunto, if it shall please the company of stationers in London to send hither some certain men from them with sufficient authority for that purpose. Thus most humbly desiring that the press may no longer be stayed, and hoping that your honour will further our desire herein, we do in our daily prayer commend your lordship to the blessed tuition of the Almighty.

From Cambridge, this 14th of June[1].

This letter has been quoted in full partly because it is the first of a long series of protests, partly because it is a good example of the attitude consistently adopted by the university in regard to printing—a dutiful desire not to abuse their privilege coupled with a dignified determination not to be bullied by the Stationers.

As a result of the appeal contained in the letter, the charter of 1534 was submitted to the Master

1 Cooper, *Annals*, II, 393.

of the Rolls, who concurred in the opinion that it was valid; and on 24 July, 1584, Thomas entered into a recognizance in 500 marks before the Vice-Chancellor.

Books now began to issue from Thomas's press and some of them quickly excited the odium theologicum; when, for instance, a work by Walter Travers in support of Presbyterianism was printed, the greater part of the edition was confiscated.

Ever sens I hard that they had a Printer in Cambridg (wrote Archbishop Whitgift to Lord Burghley), I did greatlie fear this and such like inconveniences wold followe, nether do I thingk that yt wyll so stay, for althowgh Mr Vicechancellor that now ys, be a verie careful man and in all respectes greatlie to be commended, yet yt may fawle owt hereafter, that some such as shal succeade hym wyll not be so well affected, nor have such care for the publike peace of the Church, and of the state, but whatsoever your Lordship shall thingk good to be done in this matter...I wyll performe yt accordinglie. I thingk yt verie convenient that the bokes should be burned, beeing verie factius and full of untruthes: and that (yf printing do styll there continew) sufficient bonds with suerties shold be taken of the printer not to print anie bokes, unless they be first allowed by lawfull authoritie, for yf restrante be made here and libertie graunted there, what good can be done....[1]

From this time forward, indeed, Cambridge printing was for many years continually harassed by two disturbing forces—theological suspicion and by commercial jealousy. Thus, in 1585, when it was discovered that London printers had printed various books already printed by the universities, a

1 Cooper, *Annals*, ii, 400.

grace was passed forbidding Cambridge booksellers to sell, and Cambridge students to buy, "any book printed at London or elsewhere in England, which had been or thereafter should be printed at Cambridge or Oxford," always provided that the university printers did not sell their books at a higher price than that fixed by the Vice-Chancellor and the others named in Thomas's articles.

In the next year the archbishop was again growing anxious; in June, 1586, it was laid down by a Star Chamber ordinance that no book was to be printed without either his own or the Bishop of London's approval, and a few months later Whitgift wrote to his very loving friend the Vice-Chancellor:

Salutem in Christo. I understand that there is now in printing by the printer of that university, a certain book, called Harmonia Confessionum Fidei, in English, translated out of Latin; which book, for some special causes, was here [i.e. in London] rejected, and not allowed to be printed. These are therefore to require you, that presently upon receipt hereof you cause the said book to be stayed from printing any further; and that nothing be don more therein, until you shall receive further direction from me. And whereas there is order taken of late by the lords of the council, that from henceforth no book shall be imprinted either in London or in either of the universities, unless the same shall be allowed and authorized by the bishop of London or my self, I do likewise require you to take special care, that hereafter nothing be imprinted in that university of Cambridge but what shall be authorised accordingly. And so not doubting of your diligent circumspection herein, I commit you to the tuition of Almighty God[1].

1 Cooper, *Annals*, II, 425.

As the *Harmony of Confessions* was duly published
in the same year, it would appear that it eventually
received the archbishop's approval; Macaulay's
view of Whitgift as a "narrow-minded, mean, and
tyrannical priest" would certainly have been confirmed had he considered him in the light of his
censorship of Cambridge books.

Thomas Thomas's greatest achievement, perhaps,
was the compilation and printing of his *Latin
Dictionary* and when the London stationers began
to publish editions of this and other Cambridge
books, the university made another long protest
to the Chancellor, pointing out that it was a "verie
hard matter" either for the university to maintain
its privilege or for the printer to do any good by
his trade and begging of him "to become a meanes
to her highnes in this behalf...to graunt a speciall
lycence to this our Universitie."

As the Star Chamber decree of 1586, to which
reference has been already made, ordained that
"none of the printers in Cambridge or Oxford for
the tyme being shal be suffered to have any moe
apprentices then one at one tyme at the most," it
is not to be expected that the output from Thomas's
press should be very large. But we know that
before his death at the early age of 35 he printed
at least twenty books[1]. Many of these reflect the
theological controversies of the time as, for
instance, *Two Treatises of the Lord His holie Supper
...written in the French tongue by Yues Rousseau and
Iohn de l'Espine...translated into English* ("a very

1 See Appendix II.

elegant type, and as carefully printed," according to Herbert) and *Antonii Sadeelis viri clarissimi vereque Theologi de Rebus Grauissimis controuersis Disputationes accuratae Theologice et scholastice Tractatae*, both printed in 1584. In the inventory of his will it is interesting to note that, with one exception, Thomas had stock, at the time of his death, of all books printed by himself; he left, too, 39 Reames of pott paper in the garret (£8) and 8 skynnes of parchment ruled with read ynck (2s 8d). His serviceable type, consisting of long primer, pica, and brevier (Roman and Italique), together with some "greeke letter," amounted to 1445 lb and was valued at 3d a lb. In his "necessaries for pryntinge" are included "one presse with the furneture" (66s 8d), "iiijᵒʳ payer of chases" (13s 4d), "ij great stooles" (12d), "iiijᵒʳ gallies" (16d) and "the wasshing troufhe" (12d)[1].

But it is on his *Latin Dictionary* that the fame of Thomas Thomas chiefly rests. "In hoc opere" he writes on the title-page, "quid sit praestitum ad superiores λεξικογραφοὺς adjectum, docebit epistola ad Lectorem" and in the *epistola* we learn how the work came into being:

Precibus enim Ludimagistrorum ac studiosorum victus, quibus accessit etiam amicorum frequens postulatio, ex immenso Lexicorum pelago nostrum contraxi, quod trivialibus saltem ludis inserviret.

The last words of this same address to the reader show that, like Johnson's, the dictionary was not

[1] Gray and Palmer, *Wills of Cambridge Printers*, pp. 70, 71.

compiled "in the soft obscurities of retirement, or under the shelter of academick bowers":

Cantebrigiae ex nostris aedibus, carptim inter operarum susurros, Tertio Nonas Septembres, Anno salutis per Christum Dominum partae, 1587.

In the eleventh edition, printed by Thomas's successor in 1619, the following tribute is paid to him in the dedication to Francis Bacon:

He was about 30 years ago a famous Printer among your Cantabrigians; yes something more than a Printer such as we now are, who understand the Latin that we print no more than Bellerophon the letters he carried, and who sell in our shops nothing of our own except the paper *black with the press's sweat.* But he, a companion of the Stephenses and of the other, very few, printers of the true kind and best omen, was of opinion that it was men of learning, thoroughly imbued with academic studies, who should give themselves to cultivating and rightly applying that illustrious benefit sent down from heaven and given to aid mankind and perpetuate the arts. Accordingly what more fit than that when he had wrought what was worthy of type, he should himself, needing aid of none, act as midwife to his own progeny.

Thomas's printing-office was in the Regent Walk, immediately opposite the west door of Great St Mary's; his death is said to have been hastened by the labours of the dictionary, and in 1588 he was buried in the churchyard of Great St Mary's.

ORNAMENT USED BY THOMAS THOMAS

III

FROM JOHN LEGATE TO
ROGER DANIEL

NO time was lost, after the death of Thomas Thomas, in appointing a successor, for John Legate was elected by grace of 2 November, 1588, "as he is reported to be skilful in the art of printing books"; and almost immediately the new printer became involved in disputes with the Stationers' Company.

The corporate existence of the London Stationers dates back to 1407, but their first charter was granted by Mary in 1557. The result of this charter of incorporation was that no one, except the holders of special licences or privileges, could print books for sale; by the rules of the company a member who wished to print a book and claim the ownership of it was required to enter its name in the register of the company. Thus he obtained the only kind of 'copyright' which then existed.

On her accession, Elizabeth confirmed the Stationers' charter, but shortly afterwards, *Injunctions* were issued which required all books to be licensed either by the Queen herself, or six members of the Privy Council, or the Archbishops, or the Bishop of London, or the Chancellors of the Universities, or the bishop of the diocese.

It was, however, found to be impossible to enforce such a stringent regulation and in 1577 we find a number of printing licences issued to private persons. Thus John Jugge became Her Majesty's printer of Bibles; to Richard Tothill was given the "printinge of all kindes *Lawe bookes*"; to John Day the monopoly of the *ABC* and *Catechism*; to Thomas Marshe "Latin books used in the grammar schools"; to William Seres "salters, primers and prayer books."

As we have already seen, it was these grants which, in spite of the confirmation of the university's licence at the beginning of the reign, effectually stood in the way of the establishment of a press at Cambridge by John Kingston.

The London Stationers also took alarm and petitioned the Queen. At first they were merely rebuked for daring to question the royal prerogative but, "approaching her Majesty a second time more humbly than before," the Company was granted a monopoly of both printing and selling psalters, primers, almanacks, *ABC*'s, the little Catechism, and Nowell's English and Latin Catechism.

Of all such monopolies the university, by the power given to it in the charter of 1534 to print *omnimodos libros*, had been made nominally independent, and it was therefore inevitable that disputes should arise; furthermore, there being as yet no regularised law of copyright, such disputes were likely to be most violent when there was competition in the sale, as well as in the printing, of a text-book.

Thus when John Legate, himself a freeman of the Stationers' Company, printed an edition of Terence for the use of scholars in 1589 and sent copies to be sold in London, the Stationers quickly confiscated them; on their part, the Stationers were at the same time contemplating another pirated edition of Thomas's *Dictionary*. The university made its usual, dignified complaint to Lord Burghley.

Again, in 1591, Legate, who had in that year produced the first English bible printed at Cambridge, was accused of infringing the monopoly of Barker and Day, the privileged printers. In their reply to the charge, the Vice-Chancellor and Heads of Houses whilst hinting that the doctrine "that the prince by virtue of prerogative may, by a later grant, either take away or abridge a former" is not only "against the rule of natural equity" but also "dangerous to all degrees, opening a way to the overthrow of all patents and privileges," base their appeal upon an *ad misericordiam*, with a final reminder of the charter and its ratification; in particular, they emphasise the plight of the printer himself:

The suit which they [the Stationers] have made unto your lordship for the stay of our printer until the next term, is so prejudicial to the poor man, as if they should prevail therein, it could not but tend to his utter undoing; especially Sturbridge-fair now drawing near; being the chiefest time wherein he hopeth to reap greatest fruit of this his travail[1].

Similarly, in 1596, Legate was charged—this time by the Ecclesiastical Commissioners—with infringing the right of the Queen's patentees by

1 Strype, *Annals of the Reformation*, IV, 51, quoted in Cooper, *Annals*, II, 491.

printing the Grammar and Accidence. The Vice-Chancellor was required to collect all copies printed at Cambridge and to take bond with surety in £100 of each of the university printers not to print either book without leave. Some months later the Vice-Chancellor reported to the Archbishop that search had been made "by honest men sworn who said upon their oath that there were no such books printed here." This is the last we hear of such disputes for some time, but it is clear that the university jealously guarded its right of selling, as well as of printing, books, since in 1592 J. Tidder, of London, was sued in the Vice-Chancellor's Court for selling books in the Cambridge market[1].

In the later part of his career Legate became intimately associated with the London stationers. An entry in the Stationers' Registers under the date 1 August, 1597, shows that his official position was then recognised:

WHEREAS John legat hathe printed at Cambridge by Aucthoritie of the vniuersitie there a booke called the *Reformed Catholike*: This seid booke is here Registred for his copie so that none of this Company shall prynt yt from hym. PROVIDED that this entrance shalbe voyd yf the seid booke be not Aucthorised by the seid vniuersitie as he saieth it is, vj[d].[2]

Legate married the daughter of Christopher Barker and became Master of the Stationers' Company in 1604. He left Cambridge in 1609 and after that date all books printed by him have *London* on the title-page; the title, however, of

1 Registry MS 33. 2. 1.
2 Arber, *Stat. Reg.* III, 88.

"printer to the university" he retained until his death in 1620.

In Cambridge he rented a shop for 5s per annum in St Mary's parish from 1591 to 1609, probably the same house in the Regent Walk as that in which Thomas had lived, and was the first printer to use the device *Alma Mater Cantabrigia* with the motto *Hinc Lucem et Pocula Sacra* surrounding it.

In partnership with Legate was John Porter. There is no record of his appointment, but it is evident that he was one of the university stationers appointed under the charter. In 1593 we find him associated with Legate in the prosecution of John Tidder and several books of 1595 and other dates are described as printed for him and John Legate[1].

In the Register of the Stationers' Company it is recorded under the date 26 April, 1589:

Cantrell Legge sonne of Edwarde Legge of Burcham in the Countie of Norffolk Yoman, hathe put himself apprentize to John Legat Citizen and Stacioner of London for Eighte yeres from midsomer nexte[2].

This Cantrell Legge was appointed one of the university printers in 1606 and appears to have issued many books in co-operation with the Stationers. Later, however, difficulties again arose, for in 1620 Legge was prosecuted by the company for printing Lily's *Grammar*. The university ve-

1 *The Foundation of the Christian Religion*, by W. Perkins (1601), was printed for John Porter only.
2 Arber, *Stat. Reg.* II, 157.

hemently protested to the Archbishop of Canterbury:

Ferunt enim Londinenses Bibliopolas suum potius emolumentum quam publicum spectantes, (quae res et naturae legibus et hominum summe contraria est) monopoliis quibusdam inhiare, ex quo timemus librorum precia auctum iri, et privilegia nostra imminutum. Nos igitur hoc metu affecti, ubi sanguis solet in re dubia ad cor festinare, ita ad Te confugimus primariam partem ecclesiastici corporis....

and to Lord Chancellor Bacon:

Ecquid permittis Domine?...Aspicis multitudinem Librorum indies gliscentem, praesertim in Theologia, cujus Libri si alii aliis (tanquam montes olim) imponerentur, veri simile est, eos illuc quo cognitio ipsa pertingit ascensuros. Quod si et numerus Scriptorum intumescat, et pretium, quae abyssus crumenae tantos sumptus aequabit? Jam vero miserum est, pecuniam retardare illam, cui naturae spiritum dederit, feracem gloriae, et coeleste ingenium quasi ad metella damnari. Qui augent precia Librorum, prosunt vendentibus libros non ementibus, hoc est cessatoribus non studiosis....[1]

Evidently the high prices charged by the Stationers for books of which they held, or claimed to hold, a monopoly were the source of bitter complaints amongst teachers and students and the university authorities set up a spirited opposition: "As to ye poore printer," wrote Dr Gooch, Master of Magdalene, to the Registrary (James Tabor): "there is no waye but one, the universitie must stand upon our Charter."[2]

Tabor prepared a list of comparative prices show-

1 Herbert's *Remains*, 217, 218, quoted in Cooper, *Annals*, III, 138, 139.
2 Registry MS 33. 2. 23.

ing that while the Stationers charged 4*d* a sheet for Aesop's *Fables* the Cambridge printer sold them at 3*d*, that Ovid's *Epistles* cost 8*d* a sheet in London and only 5*d* in Cambridge and so on[1].

Finally, the university seized the opportunity offered by the King passing through Royston on 16 December, 1621, to bring the matter before the supreme tribunal.

Dr Mawe, the Vice-Chancellor, was in London at the time but, leaving his own business unfinished, he hastened back and with Dr Warde, Dr Beale, the Registrary, and Legge himself "went to Royston to deliver a Letter and Petition to the King in ye behalf of ye Universitye."[2] The King, having heard the complaint against the Stationers' monopoly of "ye cheife vendible books in the land," against their high prices, their bad paper, and their inaccurate printing, referred the matter to a committee com-

[1] Registry MSS 33. 2. 19, 95.
[2] Tabor kept a careful account of the expenses of the visit. The following is a typical extract:

Sunday night supper

Brest of mutton	xviijd
Salletts	iiijd
Pullett	xxiid
Larkes	xviijd
Cheese	ijd
Wine and tobacco	xvjd
bred and bere	xxd

sum viijs iiijd

Buttord Alle	ijs
Suger	iiijd
bere	xd
fyre	ijs vid

vs xd (Registry MS 33. 2. 29)

To the Kings most Excellent Maᵗⁱᵉ.

The humble Petition of yᵉ Vice-Chauncellour, &͛ Heads of yᵉ Vniuersitie of Cambridge

Moſt humble ſheweth

That whereas King Henry yᵉ viii.ᵗʰ by his Charter granted to yᵉ Chauncellour, Mᵃˢᵗʳˢ. Scholars of yᵉ Vniuerſitie of Cambridge Pˣⁿⁱ of his Reigne authoriſed yᵐ to nominȃte & chooſe 3 Stationers & Printers, & gaue yᵐ power to print all manner oᵗ bookes allowed, &͛ to be allowed by yᵉ Vice-Chauncellour, &͛ 3 Dᵗⁿ there. wᵗʰ Charter is alſo confirmed by Mᵃˣ of Parlamen xiiiᵗᵒ Eliz & is ſince ratified by yᵉ Maᵗⁱᵉ of yᵗ Highnes Raigne. Since wᵗ graunt one Mʳ Norton and other Stationers Printers of London haue procured from yᵗ Maᵗⁱᵉˢ diuers Letters Patents, by virtue of wᶜʰ &͛ challenge to themſelues 3 ſole printing & ſale of yᵉ chiefe vendible bookes in yᵉ lande. And haue alſo by colour of a Charter graȵted to yᵉ Compᵃⁿⁱᵉ of Stationers &͛ ſtrength of their decrees & orders (wᶜʰ yᵉ haue procured, or made amongſt themſelue) combined together, that none of their Companie ſhall retayle any bookes but thoſe wᶜʰ are of their owne, or wᶜʰ yᵉ haue inġroſſed from a poore Printer after 8 or 9 yᵉ Raime yᵉ yᵉ may retayle yᵐ after 2ᵈ &͛ to yᵉ great hynderance of learning & grieuance of all yᵉ Maᵗⁱᵉˢ ſubiects, who are forced by their practiſes to pay vi-viii. ſhay̋ᵐ ſome 2 parts in 3 dearer for theſe bookes yᵉ haue thus in Patent, or haue inġroſſed thᵉ otherwiſe yᵉ would &͛ might be ſold for

By wᶜʰ their vnconſcionable dealing yᵉ Petitioners perceiuing their diuerſe aymes. was to ouerthrowe all Printers, but yᵉ owne Companie, &͛ yᵉ yᵉ abuſed yᵉ whole Comon-wealth in yᵉ exceſſiue prices of yᵉ bookes bad paper & falſe printinge They licenſed oᵘʳ Printer to imprint Lillys Grammar wᶜʰ he (hauing printed amended & corrected of many groſſe faults) offered to ſell yᵉ ſame a 3ᵈ part cheaper then yᵉ did Whereupon Mʳ Norton who had (as he ſayth) procured the ſole printing thereof to himſelfe &͛ yet farmed out yᵉ ſame for 300ˡⁱ fine, &͛ 300ˡⁱ rent per annu̇ procured from yᵉ Maᵗⁱᵉ an order to reſtraine yᵉ Petitioners Printer from yᵉ ſale of his bookes & alſo failed vpon others of yᵗ to yᵗ vtter vndoeing of yᵉ poore Printer.

Now for yᵉ yᵉ benefit intended to yᵉ Vniuerſitie by yᵉ oᵘʳ Charter is vtterly taken away, & all yᵗ Maᵗⁱᵉˢ ſubiects are abuſed by yᵉ ſayd Stationers printers May it therefore pleaſe yʳ moſt Excellent Maᵗⁱᵉ to take vs &͛ yᵉ cauſe into yʳ gracious protectiȏ & eyther to ſet downe ſuch order therein, as in yᵉ Princely care & fauour to yᵉ Vniuerſitie you ſhall thinke fitteſt for yᵉ reſtoring of ſo great a benefit graunted to ſo fitt a place. for yᵉ aduancement of learning, releife of yᵉ poore Printer, & yᵉ generall good of yᵉ whole kingdome or to appoint Cȏmiteeſ to heare, examine, &͛ finally determine theſe wrongs, & grieuances wᶜʰ are moued & complained of. And yʳ Petitioners ſhall &͛

posed of the Archbishop of Canterbury, the Bishop of Lincoln, Lord Maundeville, and the Lord Chief Justice.

This committee, however, by reason of "several and distracted imployments" had no time to discuss the case and, acting on its recommendation, the King himself directed that the university printer might continue to sell his *Grammars* without the let or disturbance of any person whomsoever.

But a trade dispute of long standing was not settled, even in the seventeenth century, by a royal injunction. The leading London booksellers combined to keep the Cambridge edition of Lily's *Grammar* ("though sold at the cheapest price") out of the market and by intimidation compelled other booksellers to follow their lead; the university retaliated by a grace of the Senate which forbade Cambridge booksellers to deal with the hostile London group and ordered all members of the university "who should desire any author, of whatsoever language, or any composition of his own, to be printed, wheresoever he should live in England," to offer his work to the university printer in the first instance and further, if he should become a schoolmaster, "to use the books printed in the university which may be for the profit of his boys, and not suffer others than those printed in the university in his school, whilst the same books should be printed and sold here at a moderate and fair price by the royal authority." That the university authorities became impatient of the continual disputes both between Cambridge

May it please yo. Maiestÿ.

Having not tyme to discusse the Rights & Interests of the
University, & the Stationers, at this praesint, by reason of
o.r severall & distracted imployments; Wee are of opinion
that the poore Printer of y.e University, may, with your
Ma.ties leave vpon his peticon, sell these praesint Gramars
for his reliefe. Without any praejudice for all that to the
Title of the Stationers. All which wee Submitt
to your Majesties wisdome & pleasure./

11. Feb. 1621.

G: Cant: Jo: Lincoln. C.S.:   [signature]

James R.

THE REPLY TO THE PETITION

(With the signatures of James I, the Archbishop of Canterbury,
the Bishop of Lincoln, and Lord Maundeville)

printers themselves and between the Cambridge printers and the London stationers is shown by the appointment in 1622 of a syndicate to examine "what charters orders and decrees have heretofore been granted and made concerning the government of the University presses and the printers and the stationers and how they have been observed and when broken and by whom."[1]

The next award of the Privy Council, made on 29 November, 1623, embodied a compromise: the Cambridge printers were authorised to comprint with the Stationers all books save bibles, books of common prayer, grammars, psalters, primers or books of common law; they were to have one press only and to print only those almanacks of which the first copy was brought to them. A later order similarly forbade the printing of prayer-books, "and as to books whereof the first copy was brought to the University printer, he was to have the sole printing, as the London printers were to have of all books whereof the first copy was brought to them."

From the rather wearisome history of this constantly recurring dispute[2], two main facts seem to emerge: the difficulty, in the absence of any fixed law, of establishing copyright in a printed book and the incompatibility of the wide powers conferred on the university by the charter of 1534 with the Stationers' claim to a trade monopoly.

1 Registry MS 33. 1. 6.
2 Registry MSS 33. 2. 2–67. See also *Scintilla*, a tract of 1641 reprinted in Arber, *Stat. Reg.* (IV, 35), and Darlow and Moule (I, 189) and containing "a remarkable testimony to the never-ending competition in the book trade."

A study of the list of books printed between 1588 and 1625 will show that there was by this time a slow, but steady, output of Cambridge books. Prominent among them are the works of that voluminous theologian, William Perkins, "the Learned, pious, and painfull preacher of God's word in St Andrewes in Cambridge" whose virtues are celebrated by Fuller in the second book of *The Holy State* (1642):

His Sermons were not so plain but that the piously learned did admire them, nor so learned but that the plain did understand them....He would pronounce the word *Damne* with such an emphasis as left a doleful Echo in his auditours ears a good while after. And when Catechist of Christ-Colledge, in expounding the Commandments, applied them so home, able almost to make his hearers hearts fall down, and hairs to stand upright.

Perkins's works, dealing with such subjects as *A Direction for the government of the Tongue, Salve for a Sicke man, A Reformed Catholike*, and *The Damned art of witchcraft*, and other theological matters were collected into three folio volumes.

Thomas's *Latin Dictionary* was regularly reprinted, reaching its tenth edition in 1610.

In 1603 there appeared *Threno-thriambeuticon. Academiae Cantabrigiensis ob damnum lucrosum, & infoelicitatem foelicissimam, luctuosus triumphus*, a symposium of classical expressions of grief and joy on the death of Elizabeth and the accession of James I. Amongst the contributors were Phineas Fletcher, Matthew Wren (afterwards Bishop of Ely) and Dr Stephen Perse. Similar anthologies of loyalty were published in celebration of the return of the Prince of Wales from Spain in 1623 and of his accession in 1625, and the practice was continued throughout several reigns; a poem in Latin hexameters (*In homines nefarios*) was also provoked by the Gunpowder Plot. Two works of James I were printed at the Press: *A Princes Looking Glasse*, translated by W. Willymot (1603), and *A Remonstrance for the Right of Kings* (1616 and 1619).

In 1610 there appeared the first work of Giles Fletcher: *Christs Victorie and Triumph in Heaven and Earth over and after death*, with a dedicatory epistle to Nevile, the Master of Trinity:

My opinion of this Island hath always been, that it is the very face, and beauty of all Europe, in which both true Religion is faithfully professed without superstition, and (if on earth) true Learning sweetly flourishes without ostentation: and what are the two eyes of this Land, but the two Universities...and truly I should forget myself, if I should not call Cambridge the right eye.

In the same year there was printed for David Owen, Fellow of Clare Hall, a controversial work entitled *Herod and Pilate reconciled*. This led Ralph Brownrigg (Fellow of Pembroke and afterwards Bishop of Exeter) to invite Owen to his rooms and to catechise him as to whether a king breaking fundamental laws might be opposed. The Vice-Chancellor thereupon summoned Brownrigg to Trinity and after reminding him that Owen's book had received official sanction to be printed, suspended him from his degrees both for questioning the university's privilege of printing and for propounding seditious questions to Owen. Brownrigg recanted shortly afterwards and was restored by the Vice-Chancellor, but the incident is interesting, as showing the jealousy with which the privilege of university printing was guarded and the limitations imposed upon free speech even in college rooms.

More serious trouble arose out of the publication of a controversial work entitled *The Interpreter* by John Cowell, Master of Trinity Hall. It was suppressed by royal proclamation in 1610 and all copies were ordered to be brought to the Chancellor or Vice-Chancellor.

In 1623 Legge printed the first Cambridge book which contained music—*The Whole Booke of Psalmes ....with apt notes to sing them.*

Upon the methods and costs of printing at this time an interesting light is thrown by a document of 1622 entitled *A direction to value most Bookes by the charges of the Printer and Stationer as paper was sould*[1].

The finest paper is reckoned at 5*s* 6*d*, the lowest quality at 3*s* 4*d* the ream; the former was used for Bibles and Psalms in 8vo, for which the charge of printing and paper is estimated at 13*s* 4*d* the ream, the cheaper kind for grammars and school books, printed for 8*s* the ream ("though the Londiner giveth but 6*s* 8*d* at the most").

Evidently the writer is seeking to show that the London Stationers were making exorbitant profits on the sheets they bought from the Cambridge printers, for he goes on:

1 Registry MSS 33. 6. 8 and 33. 2. 95.

If upon the first sight of any booke printed in England you desire to knowe the chardge of the printer for paper and printinge, Looke in the Alphabett what letter the last sheete beareth, then reckon to that...for example take Legg's Grammer, the letter is O, so there are 14 sheetes in that booke...if you will allow them 10s a Reame, that is $\frac{1}{4}d$ the sheete, it is $3\frac{1}{2}d$ for the Grammer in Quires, and now the Stationers sell them for 8d in Quires and so they get $4\frac{1}{2}d$ in every eight pence.

Similarly the Stationers are accused of buying the Psalms at 12s, and selling them at a price equivalent to £1 17s the ream.

Cantrell Legge died in 1625[1]. Thomas Brooke, Esquire Bedell, had been appointed some time before 1608; he evidently printed in partnership with Legge, as is shown by the title-page of Perkins's *Exposition of the Sermon in the Mount* (1608) and the document containing his resignation may be assigned to the years between 1621 and 1625[2].

Leonard Greene, admitted a member of the Stationers' Company in 1606, had been appointed by grace of 31 October, 1622. He had a shop "at the south side of the steple" of Great St Mary's and was in partnership with Thomas and John Buck; thus on the title-page of Pietro Sarpi's *History of Italy under Paul*, translated into Latin by W. Bedell (1626), the three names appear together.

Thomas Buck of Jesus, afterwards Fellow of St Catharine's College and Esquire Bedell, was one of the most distinguished Cambridge printers of the seventeenth century. He had many partners, with

[1] Registry MS 33. 6. 15.
[2] *Ibid.* 33. 1. 6.

most of whom he quarrelled, and he produced many fine books.

Charles I had come to the throne a few months before Buck's appointment and on the occasion of the new king's proclamation loyal Cambridge had spent 9*s* 4*d* for "a gallon of sacke and 2 gallons of Clarrett," 5*s* "for sugercakes" and 6*s* "for a bone fier that night." Immediately after his accession Charles issued a proclamation "to inhibit the sale of Latin books reprinted beyond the seas, having been first printed in Oxford or Cambridge"—a further illustration of the evils which arose out of the laxity of copyright. But a document of much greater importance in the history of Cambridge printing was the charter granted to the university in 1628: the King, in an attempt to settle the controversy once and for all, ratified the grant made by Henry VIII and declared that the university stationers and printers might print and sell any books which he or his two predecessors had licensed any person or body of persons to sell; and, further, that they might print and sell all books which had been, or should be, allowed by the Chancellor, "any letters patent, or any prohibition, restraint, clause, or article, in any letters patent whatsoever, notwithstanding."

In spite of this, we find an order of the Privy Council in 1629 recognising the right of the university to print bibles which should contain the liturgy and the psalms, but not to print "these alone without the bibles"; further, the university's output of Lily's *Grammar* was limited to 3000 copies a year and a few years later the university appears to have surrendered its right to print bibles, almanacks, and Lily's *Grammar* for three years in lieu of an annual payment from the London Stationers.

Meanwhile, Thomas Buck was vigorously extending the activities of the Cambridge Press. His first partner was Leonard Greene with whom in 1625 he bought the whole of Cantrell Legge's printing-house from Legge's executrix[1]; Greene's complaints throw an interesting light on the difficulties of co-operation between the Cambridge scholar and the London man of business:

That whereas L. Gr. beinge acquainted with the matter of bookes and printinge by reason of his trade therein for the space of thirtie yeeres almost, and Mr Bucke being unexperienced, haveing lead a students life, the said L. Gr. did hide nothing and conceale nothing from the said Mr Bucke nor spare any paines (although to the hindrance of his owne busines divers from this) whereby the common benefite of the presse might be furthered.

That for divers copies the sole printinge whereof the said L. Gr. might have had for his owne profite as he is of the Company of Stationers of London, he hath ever brought to this presse, notwithstandinge he hath but a third part therein (and some of them and the best were his before ever Mr Bucke came into the place), and besides the charge of printinge at Cambridge is deerer then at London.

One of Greene's further complaints was that Buck deserted the old printing-house in Regent Walk ("which Thomas and Legatt had successivelie all their time hired") and took instead a lease of

1 Registry MS 33. 6. 15.

"the Angell," an inn which faced Market Hill on the site now occupied by Messrs Macintosh[1].

For all the time (Greene complained) since the presse went to the Angell his [Thomas Buck's] behaviour was to me not as to a Partner but as to a stranger or servant; when ever we came to debate any matter betweene us if I did not yeeld to him he would put me off in this manner that I came to trouble him; whereas the business concerned me as well as himselfe....

Now last of all he hired a house soe farre from me as possiblie I could not be there in partnership with him....

Beinge thus wearied with uncertainties and havinge noe bonds either for partinge or continueinge whereby I might either get or save, I thought it the safer of two evills to chuse the lesse, although with great losse for the time past and hope for time to come, besides the partinge with the deerest favour of the Universitie priviledge, which I never would have doone till my death, had it not beene for the danger I was in for debt.

Finally, Greene claims "a part in the profite of the presse for the time accordinge to rate knowne by workmen for 1275 Remes printed"[2] as well as his "third part in the Bishops booke, in Almanacks, schoole bookes etc."

How far Greene was able to substantiate his claim before the university is not recorded; he died in October, 1630.

Thomas Buck's other partner was his brother John, appointed in 1625. Though he, like all

1 Oak panelling, formerly part of this inn, has been preserved. (See A. B. Gray, *Cambridge revisited*, p. 102.)

2 This amount is also referred to in Registry MSS 33. 2. 95 and 33. 6. 9 as having been printed between September, 1625, and February, 1626. From the same documents it appears that the normal output of a press at this time was 900 reams per annum.

Thomas's colleagues, afterwards found cause of dispute with him, it is interesting to note how, on Leonard Greene's death, the brothers quickly cooperated to secure the vacant office of printer for another member of the family. The following letter[1] was written by John to Thomas on 24 October, 1630:

Brother Thomas,

I pray returne with all speede to Cambridge. Leonard Greene is dead, there's a patent void and within 14 dayes a third man must be chosen. I pray be not dissartoned att it. For I have the Vice-Chancellor and ten Heads and Presidents sure to us, and they have all (I humbly thank you) promised me faithfully to prick whomsoever you and I shall desire; I think my brother ffrancis would be a fitt man to commend unto you; but if you know it to bring in Mr Barker[2] would prove more advantagious to us, I desire you to intreat him to come downe with you, or any other in London whom you best like of. This in hast. I remitt you to God and rest,

Your very loving brother,

John Buck.

Francis Buck was accordingly elected in 1630, but seems to have taken no active share in the printing business. When he resigned two years later he claimed nothing for his patent and afterwards declared:

I only did beare the name of it to do them [Thomas and John] a pleasure or benefitt; and likewise when I did give it over to Mr Daniel I thought it would be a benefitt to my brothers.

From this it seems clear that the appointment of Roger Daniel as printer on 24 July, 1632 (three

1 Registry MS 33. I. 21.
2 The king's printer.

days after the resignation of Francis) was in accordance with the plans of the brothers Buck[1].

Another family arrangement, made earlier (31 May) in the same year, was one by which John Buck demised the "benefitt of his patent of Printer to the Universitie for the terme of vii yeares to Thomas Buck, he paieing yearely the summe of lvi[li] for the same and John Buck should exercise his brother Thomas Buck's place of Bedell during the said terme."[2]

With two bedellships and two printer's patents in the family, Thomas evidently felt it better that each brother should specialise in one department.

By his first agreement with Thomas Buck Daniel promised to take

that Capitall messuage and tenement called the Augustine Fryers wherein the said Thomas Buck now dwelleth together with the printing house and all other houses yards orchards closes wayes and all other easements and commodities thereunto belonging. Except..all that chamber over the parlor commonly called the great chamber together with the green chamber and cole house thereunto adjoyning, as also two studies in the correcting roome[3].

This paragraph has a special interest in that it describes the only one of the early printing-houses

---

1 Before his election at Cambridge Daniel was already acting for Thomas Buck. The Articles of Agreement between the Bucks and Edmund Weaver (see p. 51) were written by him and the payments made by Weaver to him (Registry MS 33. 1. 13).

2 Registry MSS 33. 1. 15 and 33. 6. 15. The "gathering of mulcts and the arresting Masters of Artes in his walke and transcribing of combinations for his said walke" were excepted from the duties which John took over from his brother.

3 Registry MS 33. 1. 19.

of which a pictorial record has been preserved. The sketch here shewn is described by Cole as

The West Prospect of what remains of the Priory of St Austin in Cambridge, late the Dwelling House of Mr Buck, and now the House belonging to the Curator of the Botanic Garden. It was taken Jan. 19, 1770 by Mr Tyson, Fellow of Benet College, from a Chamber Window in that College, and just opposite to it. It is drawn rather too short at the North end[1].

The building was "just behind the East End of St Benedict's Church and Corpus Christi College."

The inventory of the goods, of which Daniel was to enjoy the free use, shows something of a seventeenth century printer's stock-in-trade:

Six printing presses, five copper plates, six bankes, seven great stones, one muller, thirteen frames to set cases on, all the poles for drying of bookes...twelve candlesticks for the presses, two frames to put cases in, six and fifty paire and an halfe of cases for letters made of mettle and one case for wooden letters, five and twenty chases, twenty gallies, fifty paper and letter bords, two tressell tables, four tables with drawers, two troughs of lead and all the shelves and formes of deal in the wool-house.

Daniel, on his part, agreed to pay an annual rent of £190, to employ but three presses at a time, and to use paper, ink, and letter "very commendable and good so as the University may receive credit and honour thereby."

---

1 MSS Cole, xliii, 260. For other pictures of the house see Cranage and Stokes, *The Augustinian Friary in Cambridge* (*C.A.S. Proc.* XXII. 53). The house was used as the headquarters of the King's army in 1647 (*Extract from certain papers of intelligence from Cambridge*, 1647). "The report is" says the writer of the letter "that it will be this night [7 June] the King's quarters."

PRINTING-HOUSE OF THOMAS BUCK

Like others, Daniel quickly found cause of complaint against Thomas Buck. By the second deed of partnership (1633) he was to receive one-third of the profits, but in the next year protested that Buck had insisted upon impossible conditions.

One of the features of Thomas Buck's career is his close association with the London Stationers. Thus in 1631 he entered into a contract with Edmund Weaver to supply him with certain quantities of books and almanacks for three years. By this agreement Buck tied himself to print only for the Stationers for this period, Weaver "sending paper and paieing London price for the printinge," and Buck being allowed to retain as many books and almanacks as were required for sale in Cambridge. The following summary shows the type of school book most in demand and the number of books supplied during the three years:

Aessop's Fables	12,000	Ludovic vir. Dialog.	3,000
Virgills	3,000	Epitome Colloquiorum	
Mantuans	6,000	Ovid, Epistles	3,000
Castalians Dialogues	4,250	Stuvenius Epist.	3,000
Apthonius	2,000	Ovid, Tristia	3,000
Pueriles Sententiae	18,000	Corderius	3,000
„ Confabulationes	6,000	Almanacks	1,560

For Buck's business the arrangement was no doubt a profitable one, but the Cambridge stationers complained that, when they wanted school books printed at the Press, either they could not have them "because alreadie they were sent up to London," or else they were obliged to pay the high prices demanded by the London Stationers[1].

1 Registry MS 33. 6. 15*.

4—2

At the time of the agreement with Weaver, Daniel had evidently been acting for Buck in London, but after three years' experience of partnership with Buck he had begun to look at the matter in a new light.

In 1635 he presented a petition to the Vice-Chancellor in which Buck is attacked as a grasping monopolist:

At yᵉ petitioner's first entrance to be printer to the University, Mr Thomas Buck tyed him by covenants and bonds of a thousand pounds to performe and keep such Covenants as he had formerly made with the Stationers of London...it will appeare that the University Presse is servant to the said Stationers and the University and commonwealth deprived of that benefit which is intended by our Priviledge....

He perceiving that I was able to goe on with yᵉ printing Psalmes without his helpe, and that I was forward and willing to print other bookes which would more honour the Universitie Presse then those schoole books which he had agreed to print for yᵉ Londoners....

He is continually defaming chyding and brawling with your petitioner, often fighting with, beating, threatning and vexing your petitioners servants, so your petitioner and they are weary of their lives[1].

Daniel then proceeds to show that it will be more honourable for the university, more beneficial to scholars, and more agreeable to the charter to have two or three printing-houses instead of one:

For so the books printed in the University shall not be monopolised but freely vented.

The parting of the Printers will beget in them a laudable emulation which of them shall deserve best....

Whereas it is a common complaint that when schollars

1 Registry MS 33. 1. 22.

have taken great paines in writing usefull bookes, they cannot get them printed but at their own great charges, It is probable that there will be cause of the like complaint here in Cambridge, if there be but one printing house, which likewise will be taken away, for it is likely if one Printer will not, another will[1].

The result of this petition is not recorded; but it certainly did not lead to the dissolution of the partnership, for in 1639 we find an elaborate agreement[2] between Thomas Buck and Roger Daniel on the one side and six London stationers (Robert Mead, John Parker, Miles Flesher[3], Robert Young, Edward Brewster, John Legate[4]) relating to the sale of bibles, service books, singing psalms, grammars and other school books. The large stock of these books printed at Cambridge was bought by the London syndicate, who guaranteed to leave sufficient copies in Cambridge to supply the needs of the university, whilst Buck and Daniel undertook not to print further copies of the books for the space of ten years without the consent of the Stationers.

From the preamble of this agreement it also appears that John Buck had assigned his rights as printer to Roger Daniel.

However difficult, not to say tyrannical, Thomas Buck's dealings with his various partners, and how-

1 Registry MS 33. 1. 23. 2 *Ibid.* 33. 1. 24.
3 Arber (*Stat. Reg.* v, xxx) notes that "in Charles I's reign there came a new development in the trade: Robert Young, Miles Flesher and John Haviland formed themselves into a Syndicate, and became privately the real owners of Printing businesses carried on ostensibly in other people's names."
4 Afterwards university printer (see p. 62).

ever questionable some of his dealings with the Stationers may have been, his name stands high in the annals of Cambridge typography. The first Cambridge edition of the Authorised Version was printed by him in 1629, a fine book with an elaborately engraved title-page. In the next year two quarto editions were produced, and these were followed by several other editions during the next ten years. Buck and Daniel were so well satisfied with their folio of 1638 ("perhaps the finest bible ever printed at Cambridge") that they posted a notice on the door of Great St Mary's Church challenging scholars to find a mistake in it, and offering a free bible to anyone who should do so.

"The *Bible*," says a document of about 1655, "was never better printed than by Mr *Buck* and Mr *Daniel*."[1]

It was about this time, too, that the encouragement of the study of Arabic in the university began. In 1626 Archbishop Usher had endeavoured to obtain from Leyden matrices of Syriac, Arabic, Ethiopic, and Samaritan letters for the use of the University Press, but was forestalled by the Elzevirs[2].

Thomas Adams (afterwards Sir Thomas Adams, Bart., Lord Mayor of London) had in 1632

---

1 *Humble Proposals* (Registry MS 33. 6. 25). The bible of 1638 remained the standard text until 1762 (Darlow and Moule, I, 182). Isaac Barrow also paid a tribute to Buck in his *Mathematic Lectures*:

He, with the loss of his health and money, took the greatest care of the University Press, out of regard to the honour of it: and with what types he printed, especially the sacred writings, all posterity will admire (Stokes, *Esquire Bedells*, 97).

2 Parr, *Life of Usher*, pp. 342, 343.

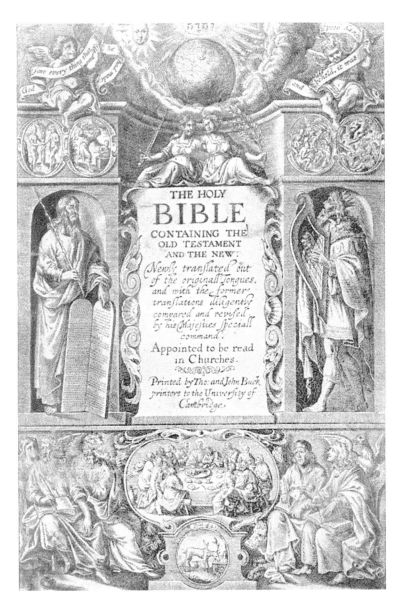

TITLE-PAGE OF THE FIRST CAMBRIDGE
EDITION OF THE AUTHORISED VERSION

founded a professorship of Arabic and some years later (probably in 1645) the Senate decreed, that having established a press and such other apparatus as should be required, they should devote their attention to the production of books in Arabic, in order that the fruits of the Adams benefaction should be handed down to posterity and diffused throughout the world[1]. There is, however, no record of Arabic printing at Cambridge until a much later date[2].

Buck was a scholar as well as a printer[3]; the edition of *Poetae Graeci Minores* printed by him in 1635, which has a title-page engraved by William Marshall, was described, though with some exaggeration, as "the most elegant book of the Cantabrigian press delivered to the public"; Mede's *Clavis Apocalyptica* (second edition, 1632) is also notable for its fine Hebrew type.

Apart from the typographical interest of the work of Thomas Buck and his partners, there are some famous names amongst the authors whose works they printed. Those of Giles and Phineas Fletcher, the two brothers who "head the line of poets who were divines of the English church," are prominent in the list. The former's *Christ's*

---

1 Registry MS 33. 6. 16.

2 Bowes, in a note on *Pietas Acad. Cant. in funere...Carolinae* (1738), says: "This appears to be the first occasion on which Arabic types were available at the Univ. Press, as up to 1736 all verses in that language were printed in Hebrew characters" (*Catalogue*, p. 121).

3 He was 17th in the *Ordo Senioritatis* of 1612–13; George Herbert was 2nd in the same year.

Victorie was reprinted in 1632 and 1640 and under the name of Phineas (who, like his brother, had contributed to *Sorrowes Joy* in 1603) we find *Locustae, vel pietas jesuitica* (1627), the poem which is said to have contributed to the inspiration of *Paradise Lost*; and, in 1633, *Sylva Poetica, The Purple Island*, and *Elisa or An Elegie Upon the Unripe Decease of Sir Antonie Irby*.

A more famous work of the period is that of George Herbert, Public Orator from 1619 to 1627, during which time, according to Walton, he managed the office "with as becoming and grave a gaiety, as any had ever before or since his time; for he had acquired great learning, and was blessed with a high fancy, a civil and sharp wit, and with a natural elegance, both in his behaviour, his tongue, and his pen." From his deathbed he sent a manuscript to "his dear brother Ferrar," describing it as "a picture of the many spiritual conflicts that have passed betwixt God and my soul, before I could subject mine to the will of Jesus my Master; in whose service I have now found perfect freedom."

This was the manuscript of *The Temple*, published in 1633, and reprinted many times in the following ten years.

Another of the 'sacred poets' whose works were printed at Cambridge at this time is Richard Crashaw (*Epigrammatum Sacrorum Liber*, 1634).

John Donne is represented by a volume of *Six Sermons upon severall occasions, preached before the King, and elsewhere*, posthumously published in 1634; and Thomas Fuller, that loyal son and

THE
TEMPLE.

SACRED POEMS
AND
PRIVATE EJA-
CULATIONS.

By Mr. GEORGE HERBERT.

PSAL. 29.
*In his Temple doth every
man speak of his honour.*

CAMBRIDGE:
Printed by *Thom. Buck*,
and *Roger Daniel*, printers
to the Universitie,
1 6 3 3.

TITLE-PAGE OF *THE TEMPLE*, 1633

historian of the university, by *The Historie of the Holie Warre* (1639).

But the most famous name of all is that of John Milton, for at Cambridge was printed the first edition of *Lycidas*. It was included in the *Obsequies to the memorie of Mr Edward King* (1638)[1] and the University Library copy contains corrections in Milton's own hand.

These few titles, selected from the long list of Cambridge books of this period, are themselves a justification of Bowes's conclusion that "the press was in a condition of great activity during the period that Buck was connected with it."

Buck, moreover, was active in university and college affairs as well as at the Press; he was Esquire Bedell from 1624 to 1670[2] and was a benefactor both to Jesus and St Catharine's Colleges[3].

Roger Daniel, as has been seen above, represented the business side of the partnership and kept a bookshop in London. Thus on the title-page of a bible of 1638 we read: "to be sold by Roger Daniel at the Angell in Lumber Street, London." Though Buck retained his interest in the Press until 1668, Daniel's name appears by itself on title-pages printed between 1640 and 1650.

1 Reprinted at the Dublin University Press, 1835.

2 His two colleagues in this office were his brother John (elected 1626) and Francis Hughes (elected 1629). By a grace of 5 December, 1664, the three bedells, "being all old and infirm," were allowed a deputy. The number of bedells was reduced to two in 1858. See also p. 49.

3 For details of Buck's activities outside the Press, see Stokes, *Esquire Bedells*, 96–99. He had a special pew in St Edward's and was buried in that church.

Sunk though he be beneath the watry floore:
So sinks the day-starre in the Ocean bed,
And yet anon repairs his drooping head,
And tricks his beams, and with new spangled ore
Flames in the forehead of the morning skie:
So Lycidas sunk low, but mounted high
Through the dear might of him that walk'd the waves;
Where other groves, and other streams along,
With Nectar pure his oozie locks he laves, oosie
And heares the unexpressive nuptiall song; in the blest kingdoms meeke of Joy and Love
There entertain him all the Saints above
In solemn troups and sweet societies,
That sing, and singing in their glory move,
And wipe the tears for ever from his eyes.
Now, Lycidas, the shepherds weep no more;
Henceforth thou art the Genius of the shore
In thy large recompense, and shalt be good
To all that wander in that perillous floud.
Thus sang the uncouth swain to th' oaks and rills,
While the still morn went out with sandals gray;
He touch'd the tender stops of various quills,
With eager thought warbling his Dorick lay:
And now the sunne had stretch'd out all the hills,
And now was dropt into the western bay;
At last he rose, and twitch'd his mantle blew,
To morrow to fresh woods and pastures new.

J. Milton.

FINIS

A PAGE OF *LYCIDAS* WITH CORRECTIONS IN MILTON'S HAND

Among the authors may be noted the names of some of the Cambridge Platonists: Henry More's Ψυχωδία *Platonica* was printed in 1642, his *Democritus Platonissans* in 1646 and his *Philosophicall Poems* (second edition) in 1647; Ralph Cudworth's *Sermon before the House of Commons* was printed in the same year.

Thomas Fuller's most popular work, *The Holy State*, appeared in 1642—a small folio with an engraved title-page on which the portrait of Charles I is characteristically flanked by the emblematic figures of Truth and Justice. A second edition of the book appeared in 1648. Other noteworthy books are the *Sermons* of Lancelot Andrewes (1641), the second edition of Francis Quarles's *Emblemes* (1643), Bede's *Historiae Ecclesiasticae Gentis Anglorum Libri V* (1643) and William Harvey's *Exercitatio Anatomica de Circulatione Sanguinis* (1649). A less important medical tract is *Warme Beere* (1641), a treatise in which are expounded "many reasons that Beere so qualified is farre more wholesome then that which is drunke cold." In 1645 Daniel printed *Tachy-graphy*, a work which claimed to be "the most exact and compendious methode of short and swift writing that hath ever yet been published by any." It was compiled by Thomas Shelton, "Authour and Professour of the said Art," and a special interest is attached to the book in that the principles of shorthand expounded in it were those adopted by Pepys in the writing of his *Diary*.

It was, however, the printing of political tracts

that brought Daniel's name into greatest pro-
minence. In 1642, "by his Majesties speciall
command," he printed *His Majesties answer to the
Declaration of both Houses of Parliament, Concerning the Commission of Array* and on 23 August
of the same year he was summoned to appear before
the House of Commons, which enjoined him "not
to print anything concerning the Proceedings of
Parliament, without the Consent or Order of one
or both Houses of Parliament." A few months later
the House of Commons again took offence at a
book printed at Cambridge (*The Resolving of Conscience*, by Henry Fern); this time Daniel was
arrested, but was subsequently released on bail,
after Dr Holdsworth, the Vice-Chancellor, had
been specially summoned to the House of Commons,
under the escort of Captain Cromwell.

By an ordinance of 1649 Parliament recognised
the universities (together with London, York, and
Finsbury) as privileged printing-places; Daniel's
printing patent, however, was cancelled, on the
ground of neglect, in 1650.

He continued to print books in London after
that date, but the petition for his restoration to the
position of university printer in 1660 does not
seem to have borne fruit.

ORNAMENT USED BY BUCK AND DANIEL

IV

PRINTERS OF THE COMMONWEALTH AND RESTORATION

THE printer who succeeded Roger Daniel, John Legate the younger, has already been mentioned in connection with the agreement of 1639 between Buck and the Stationers. Admitted freeman of the Stationers' Company in 1619, he took over several of the books printed by his father, including Thomas's *Dictionary*. For many years before his appointment he had described himself as printer to the university and shortly after the grace for his election (5 July, 1650) he and William Graves, another Cambridge stationer, "entered into recognisances with two sureties of £300 each not to print any seditious or unlicensed books, pamphlets, or pictures, nor suffer their presses to be used for that purpose"—a pledge similar to that given by the brothers Buck in the previous year.

Perhaps the most interesting feature of Legate's short tenure of the office of printer is the fact that Thomas Buck, without resigning his patent, made an agreement with him and Octavian Pulleyn by which he undertook to hand over his printing rights to the Stationers' Company of London:

The said Mr Buck shall surcease to print in Cambridge, and soe long as he shall forbeare to exercise his printing place there, that the said Companie of Stationers ...shall pay unto the said Mr Buck the summe of twenty pounds per Annum....

Neither the said Thomas Buck nor his brother John Buck shall resyne their...Patents for the Printers place, without the consent of the aforesaid John Legate...soe as the said Mr Legate may enjoy the sole exercise of Printing in the University of Cambridge....

In regard Mr Buck hath many Bookes which he hath lately printed in Cambridge now lieing upon his hand (some whereof he hath lately printed whilst he freed Mr Legate from takeing the share of the Presse in Cambridge whereunto he had otherwise been obliged) the said Companie of Stationers shall really, and bona fide, use the utmost of their best indeavours to sell all the said bookes....

For all the letter in the Printinge house of Cambridge (mentioned in founders' Bills and bought since Mr Legate was first chosen to be a Printer in Cambridge, as also the long Primmer and Pica-greeke...) the Companie of Stationers shall pay unto the said Thomas Buck two full third parts of the several prices they cost....

The said John Legate shall oblige himself soe to exercise the Priviledge of Printing in the University of Cambridge as may be most for the honor, and reputation of the said University, soe as the said Mr Thomas and John Buck may noe wayes be injured in their reputation, but may safely forbeare the exercise of their severall printinge Places in the said University[1].

This last obligation, however, does not appear to have been fulfilled, since Legate's patent was cancelled for neglect in 1655[2].

John Field, who followed him, was in close touch with the Parliamentary party. Before his

---

1 Registry MS 33. 1. 27. Cf. Bowes, *Biog. Notes*, p. 303, "He [Buck] is said to have resigned in 1653." This agreement makes it clear that Buck sold, but did not resign, his printing rights in 1653.

2 Legate's only benefaction to the university seems to have been the gift of *Annotations upon the Bible* (a two-volume work printed by him in London in 1651) to the University Library.

appointment by grace of 12 October, 1655, he had been "printer to the parliament" and had produced several editions of the bible, as well as a number of political tracts.

The London Printers Lamentacon, or, the Press opprest, and overprest (? 1660) contained a violent outburst against him:

Who printed the pretended Act of the Commons of England *for the setting up an High Court of Justice, for the tryall of his Martyred Majesty in* 1648? Or, *the Acts for abolishing King-ship, and renouncing the Royall Line and Title of the Stuarts?* Or, *for the Declaring what Offences should be adjudged Treason?*...or, *the Proclamation of* 13. *of September* 1652 after the fight at Worcester, *offering, One Thousand pound to any person, to bring in his Majesties person?* but only John Feild Printer to the Parliament of England (and since by *Cromwell* was and is continued Printer to the University of Cambridge!)...Have they[1] not invaded and still do intrude upon His Maiesties Royall Priviledge, Praerogative and Praeeminence.... Have they not obtained, (and now keep in their actuall possession) the Manuscript Copy of the last Translation of the *holy Bible* in English (attested with the hands of the Venerable and learned Translators in King *James* his time) ever since 6 March 1655[2]?

On receiving his appointment Field built a "large shop or printing-house" in Silver Street, the land being leased to the university by Queens' College. The new press stood on part of the site now occupied by the master's lodge of St Catharine's College, and served as the university printing house until about 1827.

Between 1650 and the year of Field's death

1 Field and Hills, another Republican who was his partner
2 Arber, *Stat. Reg.* III, 27.

(1668) there was, as may be seen from Appendix II, a considerable output of books from the press. Not many are of intrinsic importance, but the titles show considerable variety and a further point of interest is that the printer's copies of a large number of *imprimaturs* of books printed between 1656 and 1692 have been preserved[1]. Orders "for the better government of the presses and Printers" were re-affirmed by the Vice-Chancellor and Heads in 1655 and it is clear that the university at this time exercised a closer supervision over its press than in the days when Buck conducted his independent negotiations with the London Stationers. The specimen *imprimatur* which is reproduced overleaf shows the care with which Field preserved his authority for printing any particular book.

One of the first books printed by Field was *The History of the University of Cambridge* by Thomas Fuller (1655), who, in spite of his Royalist convictions, appears to have raised no objection to his work being printed by one who styled himself "one of his Highness's Printers."

Cromwell's death in 1658 called forth the customary *Musarum Cantabrigiensium Luctus & Gratulatio*, containing a Hebrew poem by Cudworth; whilst two years later Field, with fine impartiality, printed *Academiae Cantabrigiensis* ΣΩΣΤΡΑ, as well as two editions of the speech delivered by Richard Love in honour of the return of Charles II and a sermon by John Spencer on the same happy theme. Several bibles were printed

1 Registry MS 33. 6. 22.

25.

The Holy
BIBLE
containing the
old Testament
And The new.
Newly translated out
of the originall Tongues
and with the former
translations diligenty
campared, and revised
by his Majesties speciall
command.
Appointed to be read
in Churches.

January. 29°. 1662.

Imprimatur Cantabrigiæ

Edo: Rainbowe Procan:
Jaco: Fletewood.
Theoph: Dillingham.
Matth: Barlow. /.

Est Copia Johannis Field Tipograph:

IMPRIMATUR FOR A BIBLE, 1662

during this period, including a folio "with Chorograph Sculps by T. Ogilby" (1660)[1]. Field, however, did not (in the earlier years of his career, at any rate) maintain the high reputation of Cambridge bibles established by Buck and Daniel; for in 1656 William Kilburne presented a statement to the Vice-Chancellor showing a long list of errata in bibles printed by Field in 1653, 1655, and 1656. These errata were based upon an examination only of a few sheets and in a note at the end of the list it is stated:

If those severall Bibles were read over throughout, they would be found egregiously erroneous, without all question; And of the severall Impressions, there were about fower score Thousand printed, And all, or the greatest part of them sold by Mr Field and dispersed, to the great scandall of the Church[2].

Amongst the editions of classical authors printed during this period may be noted Statius (1651), Poetae Minores Graeci (1652, 1661, 1667), Terence (1654), Cicero, de Officiis etc. (1660), Homer (1664), Sophocles (1665, 1669), Sallust (1665).

Editions of Euclid appeared in 1655 and 1665, the former by Isaac Barrow, afterwards Lucasian Professor and Master of Trinity College.

A work which has a special interest in the history of the study of botany in Cambridge is *Catalogus plantarum circa Cantabrigiam nascentium* (1660) to which ("in gratiam tyronum") various indexes

---

1 A copy was brought to Samuel Pepys in quires by his bookbinder on 27 May, 1667. "But," writes Pepys, "it is like to be so big that I shall not use it."
2 Registry MS 33. 6. 27.

were added. The author was John Ray, of St Catharine's, afterwards Fellow of Trinity College.

Controversial theology is, of course, prominent; *Ichabod: Or Five Groans of the Church* (1663) prudently· foresees and passionately bewails the Church's Second Fall and on the title-page is a mournful female figure holding a church in her lap.

A work of lighter fancy is *University Queries, In a gentle Touch by the By* (1659). One of the queries propounded runs:

Whether if the Universities of Cambridge and Oxford should be annihilated, and the revenues imployed to the publique affairs of this Commonwealth, (Religion being now out of date, and learning of no use, where men are so generally inspired,) it is not fitting that Brasen Nose College in Oxford should be exempted from that general devastation, as a memorial of the Respect they bore to Oliver late Lord Protector.

This period was not free from disputes between the university and the London Stationers. Field and his partner had in 1655 bought from Christopher and Matthew Barker "ye Manuscript Coppie of the Bible," and the right of printing it, for £1200. In August 1662 two letters were received by the Vice-Chancellor from Charles II, ordering the university to "forbeare to print the Bible and new Testament otherwise than according to the Orders of 1623 and 1629." The university appealed against this and Lord Clarendon appointed a day for hearing both parties— the King's printers and the university. Field undertook not to publish any prayer-books until further orders; Clarendon proposed "an accommodation by way of agreement," and John Pearson, Bishop of Chester, advised the university to make a composition with its rivals. From another correspondent, who signs himself W. D.[1], the Vice-Chancellor received very different advice:

The University's priviledge is looked upon as a trust for the publick good, and theire printing of these bookes will force the Londoners to print something tolerably true...who otherwise looking meerly at gaine will not care how corruptly they print, witness the 200 blasphemy's w[ch] Mr B. found in theire bibles; & the millions of faults in their schoolbookes, increasing in every edition, so long as Mr B's composition with the stationers held...whence it was that often errors were drunk in in grammer schooles scarcely after to be corrected at the University, unlesse schoolm[rs] were so careful as to correct bookes by hand before they lett theire boys have them. It being therefore the University's interest to have youths well and truly grounded in school bookes & the interest of the whole nation to have true bibles, I cannot but think the University trustees in both respects, & feare they would afterwards rew the betraying of so great a trust if they should sell it by farming[2].

The university appears to have taken this advice and a New Testament printed by Field appeared in 1666.

Field's name is found in the St Botolph's parish books from 1657 to 1668, and in 1660 he was churchwarden.

He died on 12 August, 1668, and no successor was immediately appointed, a letter being received by the Vice-Chancellor from the King requesting that the office should not be filled for a time.

[1] Probably William Dillingham, Master of Emmanuel College.
[2] Registry MS 33. 2. 106.

At this point the names of Thomas and John Buck re-appear. In a petition to the Vice-Chancellor they repeat accusations, made against Field in 1665, both of false printing and of failure to pay sums due to the two brothers[1]. Whether the claim against Field's estate was substantiated does not appear, but it is evident that Thomas and John Buck still held their printer's patents in 1668.

The first election made after Field's death was that of Matthew Whinn, Registrary, in March, 1669; this seems, however, to have been a purely formal appointment and Field's successor was in fact John Hayes, who was elected in October of the same year, the printing having previously been leased to him for £100 a year, on the condition that there should be no further treaty with the London Stationers.

The books printed during the earlier part of Hayes's tenure of office are similar in general character to those of his predecessor John Field. Dyer describes the Andronicus Rhodius of 1679 as an *editio optima* and among the other books of the period will be found the usual congratulatory, or lachrymatory, symposia evoked by the funeral of Henrietta Maria, the marriage of William and Mary, the death of Charles II; several university and assize sermons; editions of Homer, Sophocles, Euripides, Terence, Lucretius, Ovid, Livy, Sallust; Crashaw's *Steps to the Temple* and the second edition of *Poemata et Epigrammata* (1670); John Ray's *Collection of Proverbs* (1670 and 1678); editions of

1 Registry MS 33. 1. 26.

SWAN
A NEW
ALMANACK
For the year of our
LORD GOD
1675.

Being the third after Biſſextile or Leap-year,
and from the Creation of the World (at the
Spring) 5678 years compleat.

Wherein is ſhewed the principal Aſpeſts of
the Planets, with other Celeſtial obſervations,
the beginning & ending of *Cambridge* Terms,
with other things of note in the Univerſity.

Calculated properly for the Famous Univerſity
and Town of *Cambridge,* where the Pole
is elevated 52 degr. and 17 min.
above the Horizon.

Dixit autem Deus, fiant Luminaria in Firmamen-
- to Cœli, & dividant Diem ac Noctem: & ſint in
*Signa, & tempora, & Dies, & Annos,*Gen.1.14.

---

*C*AMBRIDGE,
Printed by *John Hayes,* Printer to the
Univerſity. 1675.

ALMANACK, 1675

à Kempis, *De Christo Imitando* (1685), of Erasmus, *Enchiridion* (1685), and of North's Plutarch's *Lives* (1676); as well as bibles, prayer-books, and almanacks. The almanacks are an interesting feature of Cambridge printing at this period. Every year, under a pseudonymous heading (Dove, Swallow, Pond, Swan, etc.), a number of these attractive little books were issued.

The title-page of *Swan* (1675) is reproduced here and in *A Brief Chronology* included in the book the history of the world is summarised from the Creation (4004 B.C.) and the Flood (2347 B.C.) to the building of Cambridge (635 A.D.) and the peace with the Dutch (1674 A.D.).

At this time the printing of Hebrew seems to have fallen into disuse, as Isaac Abendana, writing from Cambridge in 1673, complains:

Paravi nuperrime versionem... sed hic desunt characteres Hebr.[1]

Hayes probably remained as printer—in name, at any rate—until his death in 1705, since there is in existence a bond of 1703, by which John Hayes and John Collyer (a London stationer) promised to pay the university £150 a year so long as Hayes continued as printer[2].

A pleasant description of the printing-house in 1689 is preserved in the diary of Samuel Sewall, an American judge who visited Cambridge in that year:

By it [Katherine Hall] the Printing Room, which is about 60 foot long and 20 foot broad. Six presses. Had

1 *Steinschneider Festschrift*, p. 90, brought to my notice by Mr Israel Abrahams.
2 Registry MS 33. 1. 32.

my cousin Hull and my name printed there. Paper windows, and a pleasant garden along one side between Katherine Hall and that. Had there a print of the Combinations[1].

During Hayes's lifetime several other appointments to the office of printer were made: John Peck (1680), Hugh Martin (1682), James Jackson (1683), Jonathan Pindar (1686), H. Jenkes (1693), another Jonathan Pindar (1697)[2]. All these appointments seem, however, to have been merely formal. They were, presumably, the last to be made in accordance with the original provision of the charter of 1534, by which the university was empowered to elect three printers simultaneously. Far more important was the arrival of Cornelius Crownfield. As early as 1694 his name appears on the title-page of Joshua Barnes's edition of Euripides of which Dyer says: "the magnificence and typographical excellence....form an epoch in the History of Greek Printing at Cambridge. It reminds us of the blooming infancy of this useful art, and the Harlem press"; and Crownfield's appointment, in 1698 or earlier, as Inspector of the Press, was part of an energetic movement to establish Cambridge printing on a new basis.

1 Massachusetts Historical Society, 1878, quoted in Bowes, *Biog. Notes*, p. 309.
2 In 1699 *The Tablet of Cebes* was printed by Crownfield for Pindar, who held one of the printer's patents until 1730, receiving a salary of £5 per annum. See p. 95.

V

RICHARD BENTLEY—THE FIRST
PRESS SYNDICATE

IN the movement for the revival of Cambridge typography at the end of the seventeenth century the most prominent name is that of Richard Bentley.

The renovation of the University Press (writes his biographer, Monk), which had continued in decay since the Usurpation, was projected by him, and mainly accomplished through his agency. New buildings, new presses, and new types were all requisite; and the University itself being destitute of funds, a subscription for these purposes was procured principally by his exertions; and the deficiency was made up by the Senate borrowing a thousand pounds. The task of ordering types of every description was absolutely committed to his discretion by a *grace* in very complimentary terms; and the power of attorney given him on this occasion is the most unlimited I recollect ever to have seen[1].

The reference to the continuous decay of the Press during fifty years savours of exaggeration. The typographical inaccuracies in Field's bibles, it is true, became notorious; but it was Field who built the new printing-house and from 1655 onwards there is no year in which the continuity of book-production is broken.

On the other hand, it is clear that the old system inaugurated by the charter of 1534 had broken down. Under that system the university simply

---

1 Monk, *Life of Bentley*, p. 56.

RICHARD BENTLEY

licensed tradesmen (who might, or might not, be members of the university) to print and sell books; and the proper working of the Press was dependent on the capabilities of the individual printer. He might be bullied by the London Stationers, as were Thomas Thomas and John Legate (the elder), and involve the university in a long series of petitions and counter-petitions; on the other hand he might make commercially profitable arrangements with the Stationers' Company, as did Thomas Buck, and disregard the interests of the university; he might accept the office with no intention of printing, but simply in the interests of a family monopoly, as did Francis Buck; or he might neglect his duties altogether, as did John Legate, the younger.

Consequently, the standard of typography, the expansion of the Press buildings, and the purchase of new type were at the mercy of the commercial fortunes of the holders of the patents.

It was with the object of bringing the Press directly under the control of the university and, at the same time, of making it worthier of Cambridge scholarship that the movement associated with Bentley's name began.

The formal initiative came from the Chancellor himself. On 29 June, 1696, the Duke of Somerset wrote to the members of the Senate:

GENTLEMEN

As I have ye honour to be a servant to you all, soe am I ever thinking of w^t may be most for y^r interest, and for ye support of that reputation, and great character wch ye University have soe worthily deserved in y^e

opinion of all good, and of all learned men: & in my poore thoughtes, noe way more effectual, than the recovering ye fame of y^r own printing those great, and excellent writinges, y^t are soe frequently published from ye Members of y^r own body; wch tho' very learned, sometimes have been much prejudiced by ye unskillful handes of uncorrect printers. Therefore it is, y^t I doe at this time presume to lay before you all, a short, and imperfect Scheame (here enclosed) of some thoughtes of mine, by way of a foundation, for you to finishe, and to make more perfect; wch tho' never soe defective at present, yett they have mett with aprobation among some publick spirited men (much deserving the name of friends to us) who have freely contributed eight hundred pounds towards ye Carying on this good, and most beneficiall worke.

Now, Gentlemen, their is nothing wanting of my part, to endeavour the procuring the like sume againe from others, but y^r aprobation, and consent, to have a Presse once more erected at Cambridge: and when that shall bee resolved on, then to give a finishing hand (like great Masters as you are) to my unfinished thoughtes, that I may be proude in having done some thing, y^t you think will bee for your service; wch I doe hope will bee a meanes to procure mee a general pardonn from you all, for laying this Matter before you, having noe other ambition, than to bee thought your most obedient and most faithfull humble servant.   SOMERSET.

The duke himself lent the university the sum of £200 towards the cost of the scheme[1] and the Senate quickly acted on his letter, for on 10 July a grace was passed authorising Bentley to act on behalf of the university and the power of attorney, referred to by Monk, gave him

1 This was paid back by 10 Dec. 1697 (*Press Accounts*, 1697).

potestatem generalem et mandatum speciale omnimoda
literarum et characterum genera ab exteris gentibus
comparandi et omnia ad idem negotium spectantia et
pertinentia pro arbitratu suo perquirendi et sumptibus
Academiae in nostrum usum coemendi.

"The commission," says Monk, "was executed
with promptitude and judgment: he procured to
be cast in Holland those beautiful types which
appear in Talbot's Horace, Kuster's Suidas,
Taylor's Demosthenes, &c."[1]

The next step was a grace of the Senate for the
appointment of the first Press Syndicate:

Placeat vobis, ut D^{nus} Procancellarius, Singuli Col-
legiorum Praefecti, D^{ni} Professores, Mr Laughton Coll.
Trin. Academiae Architypographus, Dr Perkins Regin.
Mr Talbot and Mr Lightfoot Trin. Mr Nurse Joh.
Mr Beaumont Petr. Mr Moss CCC. Mr Banks Aul.
Pemb. Mr Leng Aul. Cath. Mr Pierce Emãn. M^r
Wollaston Sidn. Mr Gael Regal. aut eorum quinque ad
minus, quorum semper unus sit D^{nus} Procancellarius,
sint Curatores Praeli vestri Typographici
        lect. & concess. 21 Jan. 169⅞.

Though Hayes retained his position as printer,
the active part in the renovation of the Press was
taken by Crownfield in his capacity as Inspector.
Crownfield is described by Ames as "a Dutchman,
who had been a soldier, and a very ingenious man";
and the earliest orders of the newly-appointed
Curators seem to have been carried out by him.

A new printing-house, facing Queens' Lane, was
built to the north of that established by John Field;

1 "52 Alphabetts, or Setts of Printing Letters, Call'd Types"
for the University Press were brought to Harwich in the
Bridgeman Sloope from Brill on 28 January, 1698 (*Press
Accounts*, 1698).

and for some years it appears that both may have been in use[1]. But in 1716 a grace was passed allotting the new printing-house (as being *Academiae alioquin infructuosum*) to the use of the Professors of Chemistry and Anatomy for lectures and experiments, and the printing was carried on at the older press at the corner of Queens' Lane and Silver Street.

The Curators' activities may be illustrated by some extracts from the first Order Book[2]:

Aug. 23rd 1698

1 Agreed then at a meeting of ye Curators of ye University-Press, y^t Mr Jacob Tonson have leave to print an edition of Virgil, Horace, Terence, Catullus, Tibullus and Propertius in 4to with ye double Pica Letter: he paying to such persons as shall be appointed by ye said Curators 12^s p. Sheet for ye impression of 500 copies: 14^s for 750; and so in proportion for a greater Number: and y^t Dr Mountague, Dr Covell, Mr Leng, Mr Laughton and Mr Talbot shall sign ye Articles of ye agreement above mentioned, on ye part of ye University.

2 Agreed at ye same time, y^t Mr Edmund Jeffries have leave to print an Edition of Tully's works in 12mo with the Brevier Letter: he paying 1^l. 10^s. ye sheet for 1000 Copies.

3 That Cornelius Crownfield have leave to send to Roterdam for 300^l weight of ye double Pica letter in order to ye Printing of Virgil, Horace, &c in ye manner above mentioned.

---

1 See Carter, 469; Willis and Clark, III, 133; Bowes, *Biog. Notes*, 314. Some of the items of expenditure upon the new Press have been preserved in remarkable detail. Robert Smith's account of 12 October, 1696, for carpenter's work, consists of about 80 items.

2 This book is, most unfortunately, not now to be found. The extracts, therefore, are necessarily taken from Wordsworth, *Scholae Academicae* (Appendix IX).

The next extract shows the executive arrangements made by the Curators; clearly the whole body (including the Heads of Houses and Professors) was too large to handle the details of administration and committees of delegates were appointed to take monthly tours of duty.

Provision was also made for the reading of proofs by competent scholars to be nominated by the editor and approved by the delegates.

Octob. 17. 98.

Present Dr James Vicechancellour, Dr Covell, Dr Blithe, Dr Roderick, Dr Smoult, Dr Perkins, Mr Barnet, Mr Laughton, Mr Leng, Mr Beaumont, Mr Pearse, Mr Wollaston, Mr Talbot, Mr Bennett.

1 Agreed y^t all resolves made at any meeting of ye Curatours for the press be entered in ye Register for ye Press.

2 That ye Major part of ye Curatours present at any meeting shall determine who shall write ye resolves then made into ye said Register.

3 That all graces granted by ye Senate relating to ye Press be entered into ye said Register.

4 That there shall be a general meeting of ye Curatours upon ye first Wednesday in every month.

5 That ye general monthly meeting shall determine, w^t persons shall be delegates for ye said Month.

6 That the s^d delegates appointed by them shall meet weekly on Wednesdays at 2 of ye clock in ye afternoon.

7 That every Editour shall appoint his own inferiour Correctour to attend ye press.

8 That no Editour shall have power to appoint any inferiour Correctour to attend ye Press, but such as shall be approved by the delegates, & y^t ye allowance for ye Correctours labour be set by ye delegates.

The delegates for this month are Mr Vice-Chancellour, Mr Peirse, Mr Leng, Mr Talbot, Mr Bennett.

Wednesday Octob. 26. 1698
1 Ordered, y^t Mr Cornelius Crownfield do go to London to procure an Alphabet of Box flourish't Letters, and to retain Workmen for the Press, and to take care for ye Carriage of Mr Tonson's Paper: and to hasten y^e return of y^e double Pica Letter from Holland.

2 Upon y^e proposall of Mr Talbot of D^s Penny[1] to be his correctour for y^e edition of Horace with y^e approbation of y^e delegates; agreed, y^t the said D^s Penny be spoken to to undertake y^e said office of Correctour.

January y^e 4th 169$\frac{8}{9}$.

At a meeting of Eight of y^e Curators—

Ordered that Mr Talbot have full power to treat about & procure a Rolling press fit for y^e service of y^e Printing house the charges thereof to be defrayed out of such money as he shall receive upon subscriptions to y^e press at London.

Agreed also that 4 pence p week for copy money be allowed to ye workmen at ye Press and half a crown p Quarter for cleaning ye Press[2].

The three following entries show that in their first few years of office, at any rate, the Curators approached their duties in a business-like way:

March 4 1698
1 Orderd, that a particular account of each Body of Letter, & of all Tooles & Moveables belonging to ye New Printing House be taken in writing in ye presence of the Delegates for ye weekly meetings of this Month, and y^t it be entered into ye Journal Book by ye person appointed to keep that Book: and y^t y^e

---

[1] This D^s Penny had been placed second in the *Ordo Senioritatis* of 1697–98 and was paid 9^d per sheet (i.e. one sixth of the compositor's allowance) for his revision of the proofs.

[2] Copy-money was the money granted in lieu of copies of books, to which the workmen were originally entitled.

said account be sign'd by ye Delegates, & Mr Crownfield ye Printer....

3 Order'd, That all Combinations, Verses, and other exercises upon Public Occasions be printed only at ye University's New Printing House.

May 3rd 1699

Ordered—that 400 lbs weight of Paragon Greek Letter be sent for to the Widow Voskins in Holland.

At a general meeting of the Curators June 7th 1699 Order'd that Dr Green & Dr Oxenden or either of them do examine Dr Bentley's account in relation to our Press, and upon his delivery of the Vouchers relating to it, and all other things in his hands belonging to the University Press; give him a full discharg; and likewise take a discharg of him for the Summ of four hundred and thirty three pounds received by him of the University.

1 At a General Meeting of the Curat^{rs} Septebr ye 6th 1699 'twas then agreed y^t Mr Crownfield be order'd to buy twelve Gallons of Linseed Oyle and a rowl of Parchment.

2 Order'd y^t ye Sashes be renew'd.

3 Order'd y^t twenty shillings per annū be allowed to Printers for their weigh-goes.

This last entry refers to the printers' annual holiday of which Randall Holme, writing in 1688, says

It is customary for all journeymen to make every year, new paper windows about *Bartholomew-tide*, at which time the master printer makes them a feast called a *way-goose* to which is invited the corrector, founder, smith, ink-maker, etc., who all open their purses and give to the workmen to spend in the tavern or ale-house after the feast. From which time they begin to work by candle light[1].

1 Hone, *Everyday Book*, i, 1133.

By 1701 Bentley's activities had begun to bear fruit.

Already (says Monk) some handsome editions of Latin Classics had been printed....Terence had been edited by Leng, of Catharine Hall, afterwards Bishop of Norwich; Horace by Talbot, the Hebrew Professor; Catullus, Tibullus, and Propertius by the Hon. Arthur Annesley, Representative for the University; and Virgil by J. Laughton of Trinity.

Nor was it only in Holland that search was made for beautiful types. In 1700 Matthew Prior was sent, on behalf of the university, to procure Greek type (the famous *Grecs du Roi*) from the Paris press. The negotiations, however, fell through owing to the demand of the French that on the title-page of any book for which their type was used there should be added after the words *typis Academicis*, a full acknowledgment in the form *Caracteribus Græcis e typographeo regio Parisiensi.* Correspondence passed between Prior, the Earl of Manchester, the Chancellor, and the Abbé Bynon, but the university refused to comply with this condition[1].

Of the books printed about this time we may note first the works edited by Bentley himself.

The title-page of the famous edition of Horace (1711) is reproduced here and a full account both of its compilation and of its reception may be read in Monk's *Life*:

This publication had been long and anxiously expected; and its appearance excited much sensation and surprise. There were found between seven and eight hundred

---

1 *Notices et Extraits des Manuscrits de la Bibliothèque du Roi,* 1787, 1, xciii ff.

Q. HORATIUS FLACCUS,

Ex Recensione & cum Notis

Atque

EMENDATIONIBUS

RICHARDI BENTLEII.

CANTABRIGIAE, MDCCXI.

TITLE-PAGE OF BENTLEY'S EDITION OF HORACE, 1711

alterations of the common readings of Horace; all of which, contrary to the general practice of classical editors, were introduced into the text....This book was, it must be confessed, unlike any edition of a Latin author ever before given to the world.

Especially characteristic of the atmosphere in which Bentley lived and worked is "the important affair of the dedication." Having discovered that the Earl of Oxford was "anxious that the world should know, that his ancestors were related to the Veres and Mortimers of former centuries, and that his family estate in Herefordshire had been in possession of the Harleys since the reign of Edward the First," Bentley took particular pains that these glories should be "fully and accurately displayed." "Good taste" comments Monk "had not yet abolished the fashion, which demanded from every dedicator, whether classical or vernacular, the most unsparing praise that language could supply."

Bentley's edition of Terence (1726) was designed, characteristically, to supplant and extinguish that of Francis Hare, Dean of Worcester. The text was corrected "in not less than a thousand places" and in every line the first accented syllable of every *dipodia* was marked with an acute accent—"a laborious task, which must have vastly increased the trouble of correcting the press." Included in the first half of the volume were a *Schediasma* or dissertation upon the metres of Terence and Bentley's *Commencement Oration* of 1725, on the occasion of the creation of seven Doctors of Divinity. The second half of the book consisted of an edition of Phaedrus and Publius Syrus, the Phaedrus being undertaken to anticipate an edition projected by Hare containing emendations "of the most daring class."

A Sermon upon Popery, preached by Bentley before the university on 5 November, 1715, and printed in the same year, is of interest not only as an expression of the vigorous No-Popery spirit of 1715, but as supplying material and phraseology for the sermon recited by Corporal Trim in the second book of *Tristram Shandy*.

It was Bentley, too, who arranged for the publication of a second edition of Newton's *Principia* in 1713. "The first impression being entirely exhausted," says Monk, "the lovers of philosophy were, in a manner, debarred access to the fountain of truth" and Bentley engaged Roger Cotes to supervise the new edition.

Into the history of Bentley's many controversies it is fortunately unnecessary to enter, but one of his pamphlets, which brought the university printer into the Vice-Chancellor's court on a charge of libel, must be mentioned.

In 1721 there appeared a pamphlet, written by Conyers Middleton, but published anonymously in London, entitled *Remarks, Paragraph by Paragraph, upon the Proposals lately publish'd by Richard Bentley, for a New Edition of the Greek Testament and Latin Version*, and full of "sheer personal malice." Bentley's proposals were described as "low and paltry higgling to squeeze our money from us," reminiscent of "those mendicants in the streets, who beg our charity with an *half sheet of proposals* pinned upon their breasts."

Bentley's reply was prompt and vigorous; he chose to assume that the author of the pamphlet was Dr John Colbatch, the Casuistical Professor[1], and answered him in what Monk describes as the vocabulary of Billingsgate. "Cabbage-head," "Maggot," "Gnawing-rat," "Mountebank" were some of the terms used. "He never," wrote Bentley, "broaches a piece of mere knavery, without a preface about his conscience; nor ever offers to us downright nonsense, without eyes, muscles, and shoulders wrought up into the most solemn posture of gravity."

This was too much, even for academic controversy of the eighteenth century; Colbatch, having first disavowed the authorship of the *Remarks*, appealed to the Heads of Colleges. This body declared the book to be "a most virulent and scandalous libel" and Crownfield was prosecuted in the Vice-Chancellor's Court for having sold it. Dr Crosse, the Vice-Chancellor, was a "quiet and timid man" and after hazarding a judgment in Crownfield's favour, adjourned the case. In the next year Bentley was cited to appear in the Vice-Chancellor's Court to give evidence concerning the libel. "There was no difficulty," says Monk, "in obtaining the citation, but a great one in getting it served upon the Master: the Esquire-beadles...were all as averse to such perilous service, as the mice in the fable were to undertake the office of belling the cat." One of the beadles, however, was bribed with a double

[1] The Knightbridge professorship, founded in 1683, was originally described as that of "Moral Theology or Casuisticall Divinity."

fee, and Bentley offered no resistance. Instead, he contrived, by an exchange with a brother-chaplain, to be on duty at St James's during the month in which the Court was to assemble and eventually the proceedings against him were abandoned.

The most ambitious work which the University Press undertook about this time was an edition of the Suidas Lexicon in three volumes folio. For this enterprise Bentley was chiefly responsible. Ludolf Kuster, a professor from Berlin, had collated three of the Suidas manuscripts at Paris and was invited by Bentley to take up his residence at Cambridge and to publish his edition of the lexicon at the Press. Accordingly on 4 October, 1701, the university made an agreement with John Owen, an Oxford stationer, by which Owen undertook to purchase an edition of 1500 copies (150 on large paper) of Suidas in three volumes at the price of £1 10s 6d per sheet[1].

The exact relation of Owen to Cambridge is not quite clear. Evidently, he was a protegé of Bentley and though there is no record of his official appointment as a Cambridge printer, several books bear his imprint as *Typographus*, including Cellarius, *Geographia* 1703; Ockley, *Introductio* 1706; Caesar, 1706; Minucius Felix, 1707; Sallust, 1710[2]. The word *typographus*, as Bowes pointed out, is used rather loosely and Owen seems only to have been the publisher of the books quoted; on the

1 Registry MSS 33. 6. 31, 32.
2 Bowes, *C. A. S. Proc.* VI, 362 and *Biographical Notes* (Errata).

other hand, there are among Crownfield's vouchers
for 1705 the following:

June 23. 1705

Then received of Mr Corn. Crownfield (for the use
of Mr Davies, and for correcting Caesars Commentary)
the summe of thirty seven shillings and four pence,
being for 28 sheets at 16d the sheet from A to Ee,
inclusive by me

£ s d   JOHN OWEN
01 17 4

Compos'd in Caesar's Commentary's the sheets Ccc,
Ddd, Eee, Fff at 8s the sheet—l1 12s od

Sept. 17. 1705

Receiv'd by JOHN OWEN

These receipts appear to show that Owen actually
was at work as a compositor upon Davies's edition
of Caesar which appeared with the imprint *Im-
pensis Joannis Oweni, Typographi*[1].

From passages in Bentley's correspondence it
also appears that Owen travelled in Holland on
Bentley's behalf in 1706[2].

But long before this Owen had found himself
unable, "through great poverty and being imprisoned on the amount of debts contracted," to
carry out the Suidas agreement, and on 8 May, 1703,
a new contract was made with Sir Theodore Janssen,
who had already supplied Owen with large quantities of paper, for the completion of the work at the
joint expense of the university and of Janssen himself, the editor's fee being fixed at £200[3].

---

1 Crownfield had also purchased a press from Owen in 1703
for the sum of £11 16s 6d (*Press Accounts*, 1702–3).

2 *Correspondence of Bentley*, ed. Wordsworth, I. 245.

3 Registry MS 33. 6. 33.

As has been noted above, however, the Press continued to print certain other books for Owen. Thus
Janssen writes to Crownfield on 19 October, 1704:

I have sent you to-day 150 Reams of fine genoa paper
which is to be for yᵉ use of Mʳ Jñ Owen when he hath
signed an agreement such as Dʳ Bentley doth require...[1].

In later years Owen seems to have laid his mis-
fortunes at Bentley's door, since, in a dedication
written by him to "Elias Abenaker of London,
Gent." and prefixed to Ockley's translation of Mo-
dena, *History of the present Jews* (ed. 1711), he
writes:

I...want Words to tell the World how much I am your
Debtor, how often you have rescued me and my whole
Family from the Jaws of Destruction; what noble Assist-
ances you have supplied me with, to raise my Fortune
in the World, and put my Affairs into a prosperous and
flourishing Condition, had not a Person of an high Character, and a pretending Encourager of Arts and Sciences,
and Printing in particular, (by the Encouragement of
whose specious Promises I was induced to leave Oxford)
been as Sedulous and Industrious to ruine and destroy
me, by such Injustice and Cruelties, which if I should
particularize, would gain Credit with few but those of the
University of Cambridge, where the Fact is notoriously
known[2].

In the meantime Kuster's edition of Suidas had
duly appeared in 1705:

Kuster (writes Monk) having now, by means of his
[Bentley's] patronage, completed the three noble volumes
of his Suidas, their appearance raised the fame of the
editor, while it excited public admiration at the spirit
and liberality of the University of Cambridge in undertaking so magnificent a publication.

1 Registry MS 33. 6. 35.   2 Bowes, *C. A. S. Proc.* VI, 364.

Correspondence between Janssen and Crownfield throws some interesting side-lights on business details—the fixing of the price and the choice of selling agents[1]:

Now that ye hurry of treating her Maj^ty is over[2] (writes Janssen) I hope ye University will come speedily to a resolution at what rate to sell Suidas, I would not have them to think of too high a price and I believe 3£ will be rather too much hoever I leave it to them but I hope they will not exceed 3£ which is 20s a volume.

KUSTER'S RECEIPT FOR A PORTION OF HIS FEE

Dr Bentley had told me you would write to some booksellers in Holl^d. Since we refused Mr Mortier's offers it might perhaps be of service but I think we could not pitch on a fitter person for disposing of a good quantity of Suidas beyond sea.

Bentley's financial negotiations with the Dutch booksellers were apparently not successful, since

1 Registry MSS 33. 6. 36, 37.
2 The university and town entertained Queen Anne on 16 April, 1705, when the conduits ran with wine and Isaac Newton was knighted (Cooper, IV, 71, 72).

copies of the *Lexicon* were disposed of to foreign booksellers by the method of exchange:

Feby 12th 170⅚. Agreed then also yt foreign booksellers be treated with for an exchange of an hundred[1] Suidas's, for a number of bookes wch shall be esteem'd of equal value, & yt Catalogues of proper bookes wth their respective prises, be procur'd from them to be approv'd of by ye University.

The succession of troubles encountered by the university both in the production and distribution of this book illustrates the difficulties of the Curators in attempting to grapple with the details of stock-keeping and accountancy. By 1732 "part of ye impression was in ye University warehouse and ye rest was got into Mr Innys's[2] hands in London, but in such manner, yt neither had a perfect book."

After some two or three years of negotiation for the mutual purchase of sheets at ½d a piece, the university, having bought the whole of Innys's stock for £400, acquired 410 complete sets of the work and appointed a Syndicate to dispose of them. The Syndics, however, found remaindering difficult:

It were well (says the writer of a memorandum of 1749) if we could get some one to take them all off our hands at almost any rate. I have tried Knapton and Whiston in vain. They durst not venture on the whole: but advise to advertize them at 30s a Book, and let ye Booksellers have them at 25s....

1 This number seems to have been increased to "3 or 400" (Registry ms 33. 6. 83).

2 William Innys, referred to by Hume as "the great book-seller in Paul's Churchyard." Samuel Johnson, in his will, left £200 to be paid to his representatives. The Thomas Johnson who assisted in the negotiations between Innys and the university (Registry ms 33. 6. 77) may have been Johnson's cousin.

I have hopes y^t Vailliant may take them all at 2 5^s a book, especially if he be allowed time for payment of the money, & ye University would take some of it in books, which we really want for ye Rustat Library[1].

Eventually, in 1752, 75 sets were disposed of to T. Merrill (a Cambridge bookseller) at one guinea each and the rest seem to have been exchanged[2]. So ended the most ambitious of the early publishing enterprises of the university.

Amongst the other books printed during this period, editions of the classics are prominent. The titles of these will be found in Appendix II and Davies's editions of Cicero, Barnes's Anacreon (1705) and Homer (1711), Taylor's Lysias (1740) may be specially noted. The edition of the *Medea* and *Phoenissae* of Euripides by W. Piers (1703) contains, in its preface, an interesting tribute to the renovation of Cambridge typography:

Si *Typorum elegantiam* mireris, gratias merito ingentes habeto *Illustrissimo Principi* Carolo *Duci* Somersetensium *munificentissimo nostrae Academiae Cancellario*, cui Cordi est *nostrum* imo *suum* denuò revixisse *Typographéum*.

Mathematics is represented primarily by the second edition of Newton's *Principia* (1713), by Le Clerc's *Physica* (1700 etc.), by Robert Green's *Principles of Natural Philosophy* (1712—an anti-Newtonian treatise) and by the *Praelectiones* (1707 and 1710) and other works of W. Whiston; biography by Knight's *Life of Erasmus* (1726); Oriental studies by Ockley's *Introductio ad Linguas Orientales* (1706) and Lyons's *Hebrew Grammar* (1735).

1 Registry MS 33. 6. 83.   2 *Ibid.* 33. 6. 86.

A work of more general interest is the first edition of Sir Thomas Browne's *Christian Morals*, published from the MS of the Author by John Jeffery and printed by Crownfield in 1716.

A COMPOSITOR'S RECEIPT, 1705

(Among the items may be noted one of Sir Isaac Newton's works and the Vice-Chancellor's order putting Sturbridge Fair out of bounds)

These, of course, are only a few titles selected from the bibliography of the period.

Between 1725 and 173$\frac{8}{9}$ there are no entries in the Curators' minute-book; the driving power of Bentley's energy and enthusiasm was flagging and

CHRISTIAN
MORALS,

BY

Sʳ THOMAS BROWN,
Of NORWICH, *M. D.*

And AUTHOR of
RELIGIO MEDICI.

Publiſhed from the Original and Correct Manuſcript of the Author ;
by *JOHN JEFFERY*, D. D.
ARCH-DEACON of NORWICH.

CAMBRIDGE:

Printed at the UNIVERSITY-PRESS,
For *Cornelius Crownfield* Printer to the UNIVERSITY ;
And are to be Sold by Mr. *Knapton* at the Crown
in St. *Paul's* Church yard; and Mr. *Morphew* near
Stationers-Hall, *LONDON,* 1716.

TITLE-PAGE OF *CHRISTIAN MORALS,* 1716

the Press had become a source of pecuniary loss to
the university. The agreements of 1706 and 1727
with the Stationers, by which the university surrendered the right of printing a large number of
school books in return for money payments, no doubt
represent an attempt to meet this difficulty[1].

Similarly in December, 1730, it was resolved to
lease the university's right of printing bibles and
prayer-books to "Mr James & Company" for the
sum of £100 per annum, an additional £5 per annum to be paid during the life-time of Jonathan
Pindar, whose formal resignation had been arranged
by a grace of 28 August[2].

This arose out of an application which has a
special interest in the history of printing.

About the beginning of 1730 William Fenner, a
London stationer,

did bring up from Edinburgh a Scotsman named W^m
Ged; who had or pretended to have found out the Art
of casting, upon Plates, whole Pages of Letters...w^ch
'twas thought would be of great advantage to the publick, as well as to the proprietors of the Invention.

This invention came to the notice of a type-

1 Registry MSS 33. 6. 39, 44. Cf. also the *Memoranda* of
Thomas Sherlock (B.M. Add. MSS 5822. 237):
They have now let their Right of printing Bibles, Almanacks etc.
to the Company of Stationers for 210*l* per annum. The money is
constantly and well paid by the Clerk of the Company. There is
likewise an uncertain Revenue arising from our Press at home, the
accounts of which are audited at the general audit.

2 Registry MS 33. 6. 45. The Jonathan Pindar referred to is
the second printer of that name. (See p. 73.) He also worked
at the University Library and his account for 1713 includes
charges for pens, ink, paper, mops, brooms, cleaning books,
scouring the brass gloab, ringing St Mary's bell, weading, and
Printer's Place (£5).

founder named Thomas James who was so much struck by its possibilities that he was
of opinion that the Design of printing by such plates would in short time be brought to such perfection as would greatly injure if not wholly ruine the business of letter-founding, by wch he then made shift to support a large family.

Accordingly a partnership was formed between Ged, Fenner, and Thomas James. The design, it was alleged, "had at that time all imaginable appearance of Success"; Thomas James, being unable to get any help from his father ("a Clergyman then living upw^{ds} of 85 years of age, who had, upon a small Endowm^{t} in Hampshire, brought up a numerous family"), applied to his brother John, an architect at Greenwich, for financial assistance. John James came into the partnership, paying an entrance fee of £100, and, as the invention of stereotype plates was likely to be used with most advantage for the printing of bibles and prayer-books, undertook to apply for a licence to the University of Cambridge —"the only one at that time unemploied."[1]

This application was successful and the lease was granted to Fenner on 23 April, 1731; Fenner's name was used as that of the only member of the partnership who was a stationer, and John James gave a bond for £100.

The plates were at first made in London, at a house in Bartholomew Close, but in the summer of

[1] Ged had previously won a wager from William Caslon, the famous type-founder; each had been given a page of type and allowed eight days to produce a plate, and the umpire had decided in Ged's favour.

1732 a house was hired in Cambridge and all the materials and implements moved thither. "For yᵉ better prosecuting the Affair," a certain James Watson was sent to Holland "as well as to hire Men, as to buy Presses" and several Dutchmen were employed in printing the nonpareil bible and the small book of common prayer by the new process.

But the business did not prosper. Ged quarrelled with Fenner and "left the whole business at a stand, Secreting or taking with him several Tools and other things to which he had no Right"[1]; Baskett, the king's printer, filed a Bill in Chancery against Fenner for printing bibles; the injunction was subsequently withdrawn, but meanwhile John James was losing confidence in the scheme and growing anxious about his money; he urged Fenner to "go on with the Cambridge Patent Work in common Type Way by the Assistance of Mr Watson, *and have nothing farther to do in the Plate Way.*" "As far as I can learn," wrote James in another letter (28 Nov. 1732), "the Booksellers all agree that the Prayer-Book that is done will by no means pass. So that to proceed farther in this Way will but run us more and more out of Pocket." Finally, Fenner died in debt in 1734; four specimens of his work in Cambridge have survived: an octavo Book of Common Prayer, Thomas Johnson's *Letter to Mr Chandler*, John Colbatch's *Examination of the marriage treaty of*

---

1 Ged's edition of Sallust, printed at Edinburgh *non typis mobilibus, ut vulgo fieri solet, sed tabellis seu laminis fusis,* was published in 1739.

Charles II, and *A Collection of Poems*, by the Author of *A Poem on the Cambridge Ladies*.

His widow, Mary Fenner, carried on such business as was left and a bitter controversy, recalling the days of Thomas Buck, arose between her and her deceased husband's partners. The brothers James declared that they were £1000 out of pocket and had received not a penny in return; that Fenner had taken a grossly unfair advantage of the lease being in his name. Mrs Fenner, in reply, maintained that her husband had borne the brunt of many business difficulties alone and that his appeals to his partners for help and co-operation had been neglected.

In their complaints to the Vice-Chancellor Thomas and John James did not mince their words:

I humbly request (writes Thomas) that my Brother and I may be heard; that so the Scene of Iniquity carried on by Mr Fenner and now prosecuted by his Widow may be laid open...for I do not find the change of Mrs Fenner's Religion has made any alteration in her morals.

As to what Fenner's wife (writes John) (who I fear is of as bad a principle as he was) may alledge, I can only say, she has no other cause of complaint, than that I refused to throw away all I had in ye world, for the Knave her husband to make Ducks and Drakes with.

The details of the controversy need not be examined here[1], but one short letter from Mrs Fenner to the Vice-Chancellor is worth preserving:

1 There is a series of 26 documents (Registry MSS 33.6.47–72) dealing with the Fenner-James dispute and the account given here is mainly based on them. Access to these has made it possible to supplement and correct one or two points in Bowes's *Notes* (pp. 315, 316). The account of the partnership given in

E I G H T
SERMONS
Preach'd at the Honourable
ROBERT BOYLE's
L E C T U R E,
In the F I R S T Y E A R MDCXCII.

By *RICHARD BENTLEY*, M. A.

The S I X T H E D I T I O N.

To which are added,

T H R E E S E R M O N S : One at the Public Commencement, *July* 5. 1696. when he proceeded Doctor in Divinity; another before the Univerſity, *Nov.* 5. 1715. and one before his late Majeſty King G E O R G E I. *Feb.* 3. 17$\frac{16}{17}$.

C A M B R I D G E,
Printed by M. FENNER, for W. THURLBOURN, over-againſt the *Senate-houſe.* MDCCXXXV.

TITLE-PAGE OF BENTLEY'S *BOYLE LECTURES,* 1735

Hon^{rd}   London 19 Jun. 1735
    S^r
        these wates on you to beg the favour you will be
so good as to stay three weeaks & then will wate on you,
in that time will Do my indaver to See Mr James & if it
is possable to bringe him to Some agreament I Rely upon
your Goodness till that time & then Shall have an opper-
tuneyty to inform your worship of my case & will do
wat is in my power to make you eassey as to the Deate
is oing to the university
                    I am S^r your
                        Dutyful Sarvant
                            Mary Fenner

Only one book bearing the imprint of Mary Fenner (the sixth edition of Bentley's *Boyle Lectures*,
1735) has been preserved and her association with
the university came to an end in 1738. In that
year she relinquished her lease and John James
agreed to pay £150 in settlement of the university's
claim upon the ill-fated partnership.

The chief cause of the failure of the Press to fulfil
the high hopes of 1696 appears, in Monk's words,
to have been the want of a permanent committee of
management, a measure which, however obvious, was
not adopted till many years afterwards. In the meantime, the receipt and disbursement of large sums of
money, as well as the necessary negotiations with persons
of business, were entrusted to the individuals holding
the annual office of Vice-Chancellor, who in many cases
possessed no previous acquaintance with the concern;

Nichols, *Literary Anecdotes*, II, 721, is inaccurate in some details.
Ged's own story of his career (which it is difficult sometimes to
reconcile either with that of Fenner or of the brothers James) is
given in *Biographical Memoirs of William Ged*, London, 1781,
and Newcastle, 1819.

a system which inevitably led to injurious and almost ruinous consequences.

This state of affairs is reflected in the preamble of the grace of 1737:

Cum prelum typographicum in usum et commoditatem Academicam olim destinatum per quadraginta retro annos ita negligenter fuerit administratum, ut Academiam oneraverit sumptu ultra bis mille et trecentas libras....

A Syndicate was accordingly appointed with plenary powers over the Press for three years.

This Syndicate "took the State of the Press into Consideration" purchasing new types, presses and other materials; and "that they might be able to retain good Hands there, by securing them constant Employment, began to print an Impression of the Bible in 12mo."

The further measures taken for the development of the bible trade will be recorded in the next chapter. Here it may be noted that one important modification of the Copyright Act, which had been finally passed in 1710, was made in 1739; in that year a new act repealed the clause which empowered the Vice-Chancellors of the two universities to set and reform the prices of books.

In 1712, 1735, and subsequent years clauses were also included in the acts imposing duties on paper by which, "for the Encouragement of Learning" the University Presses were allowed a "drawback" on paper used "in the printing any Bookes in the Latin Greek Orientall or Northern Languages."[1]

[1] In 1794 "Bibles, Testaments, Psalm-books, and Books of Common Prayer" were added to this list (Cooper, *Annals*, IV, 451).

VI

EIGHTEENTH CENTURY PRINTERS

CROWNFIELD retired from the office of printer in 1740 and received a pension from the university until his death in 1743[1]. He was a bookseller as well as a printer and seems to have done some binding as well[2]. His bookselling business was carried on after his death by his son James, and a book of 1744 is described on the title-page as "printed for J. Crownfield."

His successor was Joseph Bentham, appointed first by the Curators as 'Inspector' on 28 March, 1740[3], and elected printer on 14 December of the same year.

Bentham was the son of Samuel Bentham, Vicar of Wichford, near Ely; one of his brothers was James Bentham the historian of Ely and another, Edward Bentham, of Oxford, author of *Funebres Orationes* and other works.

[1] He was buried in the chancel of St Botolph's. His name appears many times in the parish book and in 1715 there is the following entry:
Received of Mr Crownfield from ye year 1708 seven shillings for a piece of ground commonly called ye round O in his garden which should have been paid at 1 shilling the year for ye use of ye poor.
The "round O" was a paschal garden which supported the Easter candle. The annual rent of one shilling was paid by Hayes up to 1703. (F. R. and A. W. G[oodman], *Notes on St Botolph's Church*.)

[2] Thus in 1706 he supplied six books to the University Library, the gift of Mr Tomlinson. In his account there is an item "for ye binding and putting ye Donor's Name in each book."

[3] A condition of this appointment was that if the profits should not reach £60 per annum, the university should make good the deficiency.

Joseph Bentham was free of the Stationers' Company and Carter, the historian of Cambridge, refers to him as "allowed by all Judges to be as great a Proficient in the Mystery as any in *England*; which the *Cambridge* Common Prayer Books and Bibles ...printed by him, will sufficiently evince."[1]

Before Bentham's appointment, steps had already been taken by the university to revive the business of printing and selling bibles. Thus, in December, 1740, the Curators agreed to print small bibles (9000) price 2*s* and 1000 on large paper at 2*s* 6*d*, and six months later 11,000 small nonpareil bibles and 1000 on large paper.

The services of Charles Bathurst, of London, were secured as agent and from 1738 to 1744 he was engaged in "buying, procuring, and expediting Paper, Types, Servants, and other necessaries."

Bathurst's memorandum of 1751, though an *ex parte* statement, throws an interesting light on printing conditions at Cambridge:

The Insolvency (he writes) of the University's late Lessees for Bibles and the wishes and power of the King's Printer considered, it was then a prevailing opinion, that no advantage could well be made by printing Bibles and Com. Prayers: therefore the Syndics were very diffident and cautious in undertaking other Impressions[2].

However, having previously passed a resolution that Bentham was to sell no bibles without authority from one of themselves, the Syndics in March, 174¾, covenanted with Bathurst that he should be the sole

---

1 The most important bible printed by Bentham was that of 1762, the 'standard' edition prepared by Dr T. Paris.

2 Registry MS 33. 7. 7.

selling agent for all books printed at Cambridge. Several
editions of the bible and prayer-book were put in
hand and subsequently reprinted, "but not near so
fast as they were sold." Bathurst grew impatient: " If
two presses will not do," he wrote to the Vice-Chancellor, "[I hope that] three shall [be] employ'd in it:
for truly the jests People make here of the negligence
of our Advantage and Honour are very irksome."
The university, on the other hand, found itself unable to make the necessary outlay of money for paper.
Bathurst had, according to his own account, spent considerable sums in the purchase of type and had made
a six weeks' voyage to Holland in 1747 to procure
a good stock of paper. One parcel was duly received
by Bentham at Cambridge, but by the time that the
second consignment arrived, a new Vice-Chancellor
(Dr Parris, Master of Sidney Sussex College) had
taken office and the paper was promptly returned.

I have returned your paper again (wrote the Vice-
Chancellor) which yet I would not have done, if we had
either wanted it, or had money left to have paid for it....
The Welsh Bible is paid for within a trifle: works of
authors bring in but a trifle: our chief dependance must
be on what our books in your hands produce....I am
reduced to yᵉ necessity of either returning your paper,
or, what is still worse, putting an intire stop to yᵉ press[1].

A fresh arrangement was therefore proposed by
which Bathurst should pay ready money for books
printed and the university should not be required to
advance money to carry on the business.

Another source of trouble both to the Press and
to Bathurst during this period was a second attack

1 Registry MS 33. 7. 4.

made by Baskett, the king's printer, upon the rights of the university.

In 1741 the Syndics had printed for Bathurst an *Abridgement of the Laws of Excise*, and on its publication Baskett obtained an injunction to stop its sale. Litigation dragged on until 1758, when the Court of King's Bench decided in favour of the university, declaring that it was entrusted with "a concurrent Authority to print Acts of Parliament and Abridgements by letters patent of K. Hen. VIII and K. Charles I."

Dyer says of Bentham that "he was not eager after money in the way of business, but rather ambitious of printing Works that would do him credit. He had a great taste for Gardening and a turn for humour. He was an amiable man, as all the Benthams were; and was the only Bentham of the family that was not in orders. There were six brothers, who all used to assemble at the Prebendal-house in Ely at Christmas."[1] Joseph was an alderman of Cambridge and lived in a house adjoining the Press in Silver Street, the whole group of buildings forming "a sort of Quadrangle or Square." This house had belonged to Matthew Stokes, Registrary from 1558 to 1591, and Cole refers to the arms ("carved very handsomely and very large") over the chimney-piece in the parlour[2].

Of the books printed by Bentham the most sumptuous is *The History of Ely Cathedral* by his brother,

---

1 Nichols, *Literary Anecdotes*, VIII, 451.

2 MSS 5809. 38. The coat of arms to which Cole refers now hangs in the University Press.

James Bentham, a large volume illustrated with many engravings and published in 1765.

Other illustrated works of some interest are Zachary Grey's edition of Samuel Butler's *Hudibras* (1774) with a "set of new cuts" by Hogarth and *Cantabrigia Depicta* (1763)[1]. There may also be noted a Latin version of Pope's *Ode on St Cecilia's Day* and a succession of Seatonian prize poems by Christopher Smart; a volume of *Odes* (1756) by William Mason; Roger Long's *Astronomy* (1744); Robert Masters's *History of the College of Corpus Christi* (1752); a Latin version (anonymously published) of Gray's *Elegy* by Christopher Anstey and W. H. Roberts, Provost of Eton: and many editions of the classics, including Squire's *Plutarch de Iside et Osiride* (1744), Taylor's *Demosthenes* (various years) and Richard Hurd's *Horace* (1757).

In 1715, when James Gibbs presented his design for "the Publick Building at Cambridge," his plans included provision for the printing-house above the Registrary's office in the southern wing; and it has been therefore inferred that the printing-house in Silver Street was not adequate to the needs of the university[2]. Only a portion of Gibbs's scheme (the Senate House) was carried out and in 1762 the Syndics of the Press, seeking fresh accommodation,

1 Cambridge is depicted in rosy colours:
The Air is very healthful, and the Town plentifully supplied with excellent Water...Nor is it better supplied with Water, than it is with other Necessaries of life. The purest Wine they receive by the Way of *Lynn*...Firing is cheap; Coals from Seven-pence to Nine-pence a Bushel.

2 Willis and Clark, III, 134. Gibbs's complete design is shown on the title-page reproduced opposite p. 99.

purchased a house, called *The White Lion*, which probably stood on the south side of Silver Street, facing the old Press. This was the first step taken in the acquisition of the present site.

Bentham continued in office until 1766 and well maintained the typographical reputation of the Press, but a more famous name is that of John Baskerville. Originally a writing-master at Birmingham where, from 1733 to 1737, he was teaching at a school in the Bull Ring, he afterwards took up, with great success, the trade of japanning and in 1750 began his experiments in type-founding. He set his mind to the improvement of type, press, paper, and method of printing:

It is not my desire (he wrote in the preface to his *Milton*, 1757) to print many books, but such only as are books of Consequence, and which the public may be pleased to see in an elegant dress, and to purchase at such a price as will repay the extraordinary care and expense that must necessarily be bestowed upon them.... If this performance shall appear to persons of judgment and penetration in the Paper, Letter, Ink, and Workmanship to excel; I hope their approbation may contribute to procure for me what would indeed be the extent of my Ambition, a power to print an Octavo Common-Prayer Book, and a Folio Bible.

This ambition was fulfilled by Baskerville's getting into touch with the university. In 1757 he sent a specimen of type to a friend at Cambridge, explaining that

the size is calculated for people who begin to want Spectacles but are ashamed to use them at Church....If I find favour with the University, & they give me a Grant to print an Edition of a prayer book according to

JOHN BASKERVILLE

the specimen I would...send to Cambridge two presses, Workmen & all other requisites, but should be glad to take the chance of the Edition to my self, & make the University such Considerations as they should think fit to prescribe....My highest Ambition is to print a folio Bible, with the same letter of the inclosed Specimen.

The application was successful and on 15 December, 1758, an agreement was made with the university by which Baskerville was to have leave to print a folio bible and two octavo common-prayer books, and on the following day Baskerville was duly elected to be "one of the Stationers & Printers" of the university for ten years, securities for £500 each being given by Baskerville himself and by John Eaves, a toymaker of Birmingham.

The conditions imposed upon the new printer were strict: he was to print in Cambridge only such books as the Syndics gave him leave to print; on the title-page of no other book was he to describe himself as Printer to the University; inspectors appointed by the Syndics were to have free access to his printing-office; and Baskerville was to pay the university £20 for every 1000 of the 8vo common-prayer. On 31 May, 1759, Baskerville wrote from Birmingham to the Vice-Chancellor:

Sir,

I have at last sent everything requisite to begin the Prayer Book at Cambridge. The Bearer Mr Tho. Warren is my Deputy in conducting the whole. I have ordered him to inform you of every step he takes, and to desire you would appoint a person to tell out the number of sheets before they go to press and again before they are packed up for Birmingham. Mr Bentham will inform you how many sheets per 1000 are allowed for wast. I have attempted several ornaments, but none of them please me so well as the specimen; which I hope will be approved by you and the Gentlemen of the Syndick. I propose printing off 2000 the first impression, but only 1000 of the State holidays &c which the patentee has left out. The paper is very good and stands me in 27 or 28 shillings the Ream.

I am taking great pains, in order to produce a striking title-page & specimen of the Bible which I hope will be ready in about six weeks. The importance of the work demands all my attention; not only for my own (eternal) reputation; but (I hope) also to convince the world, that the University in the honour done me has not intirely misplaced their Favours.

You will please to accept & give my most respectful duty to the University, particularly to the Gentlemen of the Syndick. I should be very happy if I could make an Interest to a few Gent^n. to whom the work would not be disagreeable, to survey the sheets, after my people had corrected them as accurately as they are able, that I might, if possible, be free from every error of the press; for which I would gladly make suitable acknowledgements. I procured a sealed copy of the Common prayer with much trouble and expense from the Cathedral of Litchfield, but found it the most inaccurate and ill printed book I ever saw: so that I returned it with thanks[1].

Evidently neither the university nor Bentham was willing to give Baskerville a free hand. Bentham was naturally jealous of his own position and the Syndics' previous experience of leases granted to outside printers had been unfortunate. Reed's criticism is therefore a little too harsh: "This learned body," he writes, "appear to have been influenced in the transaction more by a wish to fill their own coffers than by a desire to promote the interests

1 Registry MS 33. 7. 17.

of the Art; and the heavy premiums exacted from Baskerville for the privilege thus accorded effectually deprived him of any advantage whatever in the undertaking."[1]

By a further agreement of 3 July, 1761, Baskerville undertook to pay £12 10s 0d per 1000 for the 4000 copies to be printed of the 12mo Common Prayer and in a letter of 2 November, 1762, he wrote in a dismal strain to Horace Walpole:

The University of Cambridge have given me a Grant to print there 8vo. & 12mo. Common prayer Books; but under such Shackles as greatly hurt me. I pay them for the former twenty, & for the latter twelve pound ten shillings the thousand, & to the Stationers Company thirty two pound for their permission to print one Edition of the Psalms in Metre to the small prayer book: add to this the great Expence of double and treble Carriage, & the inconvenience of a Printing House an hundred Miles off. All this Summer I have had nothing to print at Home. My folio Bible is pretty far advanced at Cambridge, which will cost me near £2000 all hired at 5 p Cent. If this does not sell, I shall be obliged to sacrifice a small Patrimony which brings me in [£74] a Year to this Business of printing; which I am heartily tired of & repent I ever attempted. It is surely a particular hardship that I should not get Bread in my own Country (and it is too late to go abroad) after having acquired the Reputation of excelling in the most useful Art known to Mankind; while every one who excels as a Player, Fidler, Dancer &c not only lives in Affluence but has it [in] their power to save a Fortune.

However, four prayer-books (two with long lines and two in double column) were produced by Bas-

1 Reed, *Old English Letter Foundries*, p. 276 (quoted in Straus and Dent, *John Baskerville*, p. 46).

The L I T A N Y.

keeper, giving him the victory over all his enemies;

We befeech thee to hear us, good Lord.

That it may pleafe thee to blefs and preferve her Royal Highnefs the Princefs Dowager of *Wales,* and all the Royal Family;

We befeech thee to hear us, good Lord.

That it may pleafe thee to illuminate all Bifhops, Priefts, and Deacons, with true knowledge and underftanding of thy Word; and that both by their preaching and living they may fet it forth, and fhew it accordingly;

We befeech thee to hear us, good Lord.

That it may pleafe thee to endue the Lords of the Council, and all the Nobility, with grace, wifdom, and underftanding;

We befeech thee to hear us, good Lord.

That it may pleafe thee to blefs and keep the Magiftrates; giving them grace to execute juftice, and to maintain truth;

We befeech thee to hear us, good Lord.

That it may pleafe thee to blefs and keep all thy people;

We befeech thee to hear us, good Lord.

That it may pleafe thee to give to all nations unity, peace, and concord;

We befeech thee to hear us, good Lord.

That it may pleafe thee to give us an heart to love and dread thee, and diligently to live after thy commandments;

We befeech thee to hear us, good Lord.

That it may pleafe thee to give to all thy people increafe of grace, to hear meekly thy Word, and to receive it with pure affection, and to bring forth the fruits of the Spirit;

We befeech thee to hear us, good Lord.

That it may pleafe thee to bring into the way of truth,

kerville in 1760 and of these two were reprinted in the following year; the folio bible appeared in 1763.

In spite of their failure from the commercial point of view, Baskerville's prayer-books and bible were recognised as something finer than, or at any rate as something different in kind from, what had been produced before. Dibdin called the bible "one of the most beautifully printed books in the world" and called special attention to the title-page as having "all the power and brilliancy of copper-plate." The contrast, too, between the dignified design of Baskerville's title-pages and the conventionally crowded title-page of the period has also been duly emphasised[1].

On the other hand, Baskerville's type has been criticised as being modelled too closely upon his own mastery of penmanship—the upstrokes very thin, the downstrokes very thick, the serifs very fine[2]. Controversy apart, Baskerville's is without doubt the most distinguished typographical work associated with the University Press in the eighteenth century.

Depressed by the financial failure of his bible, Baskerville printed no more in Cambridge after 1763[3]; when he died twelve years later, a French society bought his types and used them for an edition of Voltaire and other works.

Bentham continued to hold the office of printer until 1766. On 13 December of that year he resigned and John Archdeacon, an Irishman, was elected in his place, his salary being fixed two years later at £140

1 Straus and Dent, p. 50.   2 Pollard, *Fine Books*, p. 300.
3 Mr G. J. Gray has discovered that Baskerville lived in the Old Radegund Manor House in Jesus Lane.

a year. Archdeacon had been appointed Inspector of the Press two months before, and, as appears from certain passages in Nichols's *Literary Anecdotes*[1], had been associated with a scheme by which Bowyer had contemplated taking over the management of the University Press:

In consequence (writes Nichols) of overtures from a few respectable friends at Cambridge, Mr Bowyer had some inclination, towards the latter end of 1765, to have undertaken the management of the University Press, by purchasing a lease and their exclusive privileges, by which for several years they had cleared a considerable sum. To accomplish this he took a journey to Cambridge; and afterwards sent the Compiler of these Anecdotes to negotiate with the Vice-Chancellor. The treaty was fruitless; but he did not much regret the disappointment.

Evidently it was intended that Archdeacon should be the printer under Bowyer's management, since Nichols wrote to Bowyer in September, 1765:

I write to you now from the house of Mr Labutte[2], with whom I have dined, and who has most obligingly shewn me all in his power. Mr Archdeacon is not at home. I have opened to Mr Labutte my plan, who is of opinion something may be done. I have talked also with a *Compositor*, who is sensible, and who now works in the house. *Six hundred* a year I believe may carry it. They *talk* of *ten* having been *offered*. For 7 years last past the University have *cleared one-thousand-three-hundred pounds* annually; besides farming the *Almanack*

1 Vol. II, pp. 458 ff.
2 René La Butte, one of Bowyer's printers who came to Cambridge with Walker and James, the founders of *The Cambridge Journal*, the first Cambridge newspaper; through the influence of Conyers Middleton, La Butte was established as a French teacher in Cambridge; Bentham printed his *French Grammar* (2nd ed.) in 1790.

(200 l. more). This might at least be *doubled by opening
the trade* in new channels. If any bookseller of reputation would enter into a scheme with you, *an immense
fortune would certainly be raised....*
and Bowyer, in his reply, wrote:

Mr Archdeacon, as you observe, must be a leading
person, and there is some delicacy necessary to be shewn

This proposal, however, came to nothing, and no
university documents relating to it have been pre-

From the business point of view, the printing and
selling of bibles and prayer-books no doubt continued to be the most important branch of Archdeacon's activities. In a collection of agents' accounts
for the years 1766 and 1767 the well-known names
of Edward Dilly, John Rivington, James Waugh,
T. and J. Merrill appear. One of these accounts,
made out in Archdeacon's own hand[1], is reproduced here as showing the numbers and prices of
bibles supplied to Rivington during the period of
six months and also the way in which the accounts
were examined and approved by the Syndics of the

In the year following that of Archdeacon's appointment a contract, similar to those of 1706 and
1727, was made with the Stationers' Company by
which the Stationers, in return for an annual payment of £500, were granted the right of printing a
large number of books (including school editions of
classical authors, Lily's Grammar, Almanacks, Gra-

1 Archdeacon requests Mr Rivington to return it after

R.   8

1767.

April 28 ✓ Com. Prayers folio demy 28₇ ... 55 + 8 ... 19 4 ...
May 7 ✓ Do ... 27₅
April 28 ✓ Psalms to Do. ... 28 × 2 ... 2 9 ...

April 3 & 5. ✓ Com. Prayers folio fine & two d. 28 × 15 ... 18 7 6
28. ✓ Psalms to Do. ... 7 × 4 ... 1 4 6
28 ✓ Com. Prayers 4to demy ... 55 × 6 ... 12 : 6

28 ✓ Com. Prayers 8vo demy 110
Aug. 3 ✓ Do ... 110 } 275 × 1 8 20
Sept. 20 ✓ Do ... 55
Aug. 3 ✓ Psalms Do ... 110 × 8 3 4

Sept. 20 ✓ Com. Prayers Large 12o ... 55 × 1 3 3 0
✓ Psalms to Do. ... 28 × 4 8 2

April 28 ✓ Com. Prayers 12o brevier 330 × 1 14 8
✓ Psalms for Do. & 12o bible ... 550 × 3 6

June 21 ✓ Com. Prayers Small 12o ... 550 × 9 18
April 28 ✓ Psalms Do 330
June 21 ✓ Psalms Do 550 } 1210 × 3 13 4
Aug. 3 ✓ Psalms Do 330

April 28 ✓ Com. Prayers 24o cols. ... 1100 × 6 24
✓ Psalms Do 550 } 1100 × 3 12
Aug. 3 ✓ Psalms Do 550

April 20 ✓ Bibles 12o crown 550 } 1100 × 2 96
Aug. 3 ✓ Bibles Do 550
April 20 ✓ Services to Do. 220 × 5 6

✓ Bibles 8vo crown 220 }
Sept. 21 ✓ Bibles Do 220 } 440 × 4 76 16
April 28 ✓ Apoc. to Do 55 }
Sept. 19 ✓ Apoc to Do 55 } 275 × 10 10
21 ✓ Apoc. to Do 165
April 20 ✓ Services to Do 55 × 10 2
✓ Psalms to Do 55 × 4 16

✓ Bibles 4to demy 55 × 15 36
✓ Bibles Minion 8vo 220 × 9 20 16
✓ Apoc. to Do 55 × 9 1 16

£23 13 2
Deduct Agency at 5 ℓ ℓ Cent - 21 3 8
£02 9 6

Dec. 7. 1767 This account was examined & approved
by us John Smith dep. vicech:
D. Hughes.
H. Hubbard.
M. Loop
Tipp.
John Hely
R. Farmer:
J. Brown

London Oct 13. 1767.
I have examined that accounts and
it agree with my Books. Wm Rivington

Books

RIVINGTON'S ACCOUNT WITH THE UNIVERSITY PRESS, 1767

dus ad Parnassum, Horn Book prints and Psalters) for the term of 21 years[1].

Later, in 1775, an Act of Parliament secured to the universities the perpetual copyright of all school-books bequeathed to them; but in the same year it was ruled in the Court of Common Pleas that the right of printing almanacks was a common law right over which the Crown had no control, and the Stationers' Company thereupon discontinued their payments to the universities.

However, in 1781 a new almanack duty act granted to each university the sum of £500 per annum as compensation. At Cambridge this sum was placed at the disposal of the Syndics of the Press for the publication of works of learning by the following grace of 11 June, 1782:

Cum ad graves librorum imprimendorum sumptus sublevandos omnigenaeque adeo eruditionis studium promovendum, annuo quingentarum librarum reditu Academiam nuper auxerit munificentia publica; ne aut nostra negligentia deflorescat tantus publice habitus literis honos, aut in alios usus transferatur quod doctrinae amplificandae sacrum esse oporteat; placeat vobis ut Typographici Preli Curatores in hac etiam parte Syndici vestri constituantur, atque ut quingentae quotannis librae, si ipsis necessarium videatur, vel in novas veterum scriptorum editiones apparandas, vel in recentiorum opera divulganda insumendae iis hoc nomine e Communi Cista erogentur....

Since the abolition of the paper duty and the consequent loss to the university of the advantage of drawback, this grant constitutes the single subsidy

1 Registry MS 33. 7. 20.

which the Syndics of the Press receive from an outside source.

About this time the competency of the Syndics was called into question. It was alleged, for instance, that one Syndic did not know the difference between *collating* and *collecting* MSS; a more serious charge was that the warehouse in Silver Street, acquired in 1672, was damp and that great injury had been done to the stock of sheets kept there. In reply, Dr Plumptre asserted that the damage done amounted only to £20. Archdeacon remained in office till the year of his death, 1795; in 1793 John Burges was elected printer and acted in partnership with him for two years.

Of the books printed in the last thirty years of the eighteenth century one of the most ambitious was Thomas Kipling's facsimile edition, in two folio volumes, of the *Codex Bezae* (1793), "the very crown of the Cambridge Press." Kipling was the leader of the prosecution of William Freind, author of *Peace and Union recommended to the associated bodies of Republicans and Anti-Republicans* (2nd ed. 1793), and refused to allow Gilbert Wakefield's *Silva Critica* to be printed at the Press on account of the author's unorthodoxy[1].

Gray's *Commemoration Ode*, set to music by Dr Randal, was printed in 1769[2]; Samuel Ogden's *Sermons on the Efficacy of Prayer and Intercession* (Boswell's

---

[1] Wakefield had published a Latin version of Gray's *Elegy* in 1775 and a volume of Latin poems in 1776, but left the Church of England ten years later. He was afterwards imprisoned for a libel on Bishop Watson.

[2] Cf. Cole's diary, 1 July, 1769: "Mr Gray's ode exceedingly elegant and well set to music."

favourite reading during his tour to the Hebrides) were published in 1770 and were followed by other volumes of sermons in 1777; the Parker MSS were catalogued by James Nasmith and published in 1777, the Baker collection by Robert Masters in 1784; Thomas Martyn, Professor of Botany, published a *Catalogus Horti Botanici* in 1771 and *Elements of Natural History* in 1775; the second edition of John Wesley's *Duty and Advantage of early rising* was printed in 1785 and the changing spirit of the age is reflected in a sermon of 1788 entitled *Slavery inconsistent with the Spirit of Christianity* and a *Sermon on Duelling*, by Thomas Jones (1792).

The beginnings of the study of modern languages in Cambridge are seen in La Butte's *French Grammar* (2nd ed. 1790) and in various editions of Tasso and other Italian authors by Agostino Isola, a teacher who, at different times, could reckon Thomas Gray, William Pitt, and William Wordsworth among his pupils[1].

Ten Minutes' Advice to Freshmen by A Questionist, printed by Archdeacon for J. Deighton in 1785, deserves a few lines of quotation:

It is not reckoned fashionable to go to *St Mary's* on a Sunday.—But I know no harm in going, nor that it is any reproach to a man's understanding to be seen publickly in the same place with the most dignified and respectable persons of the University.—To say nothing about the regularity of the thing, and its being approved of by people whose good opinion you may be desirous to obtain.

1 Wordsworth, *Scholae Academicae*, p. 153. See also Stokes, *Esquire Bedells*, pp. 116, 117.

It is neither my business nor my inclination to prose
to you upon the usefulness of Mathematical learning—
it is sufficient that it has its uses....
Of the standard of mathematical printing at this period
a circumstantial complaint is preserved by Nichols in
a letter from William Ludlam, author of *Rudiments
of Mathematics* (2nd ed. 1787) and other works[1]:

For my own part, I am sometimes forced to make
types, which are commonly brass, of which I here send
you a specimen ($\pm$ a $\pm$ b $\pm$ c). It is called plus-minus $\pm$.
I printed my first tracts at Cambridge when Archdeacon
(not Bentham) was their printer. I was very sick of it;
the University meanly provided with mathematical types
insomuch that they used daggers turned sideways for
plus's. They were sunk into arrant traders, even to printing hand-bills, quack-bills, &c., which they then for the
first time permitted for Archdeacon's profit. As to table-
work of which I had a deal, they knew nothing of it; and
many a brass rule was I forced to make myself....I complained of this to Mr Bowyer, and would have had him
print my essay on Hadley's quadrant[2]; but he was too
full of more important work. I remember I told him I
had marked all Archdeacon's damaged letters; which
were not a few, especially in the italic. To which the old
gentleman replied 'I don't like you the better for that.'

One of the last books printed by the Archdeacon-
Burges partnership was a translation of a Latin poem,
The Immortality of the Soul, by Isaac Hawkins Browne
who, "one of the first wits of this country," according
to Johnson, "got into Parliament, and never opened
his mouth."

John Burges continued as sole printer after the
death of Archdeacon in 1795. Two large diction-

1 *Literary Anecdotes*, VIII, 414.
2 Published in London, 1771.

aries were, amongst other works, printed during his term of office: Ladvocat's *Historical and Biographical Dictionary* (1800–1801) and Hoogeveen's *Dictionarium Analogicum* (1800); academical works of reference, such as *Cambridge University Calendar* (1796) and the *Graduati Cantabrigienses* (1800), also begin to appear; the *Calendar*, however, was not regularly printed at the Press until 1826, and it is only since 1914 that the Syndics have been responsible for its publication[1].

Finally, there may be noted Relhan's *Flora Cantabrigiensis* (2nd ed. 1802) and Harraden's *Picturesque Views of Cambridge* (1800) containing 24 views from original drawings by Richard Harraden, a London artist who came to Cambridge in 1798.

1 See *Cambridge Historical Register*, p. vii.

THE SENATE HOUSE, THE NEW LIBRARY, AND
ST MARY'S CHURCH
(From *Cantabrigia Depicta*, 1763)

VII

THE EARLY NINETEENTH CENTURY

THE immediate official successor of Burges as
university printer was John Deighton, elected
on 28 April, 1802; he, however, held office only till
11 December of the same year and seems to have
served the Press as publishing agent rather than as
printer. Thus in 1803 he, with Francis Hodson of
Cambridge and Richard Newcomb of Stamford,
undertook to purchase the whole stock of royal
octavo bibles belonging to the university (amounting
to 5627 copies in all) for the sum of £2323 10s.

Deighton had begun business in Cambridge about
1777 and removed to London in 1786; in 1795 he
appears to have returned to Cambridge, where he established the bookselling firm that has since become
Deighton, Bell and Co.

About this time the Syndics seem to have taken
counsel of, or at any rate to have compared notes
with, the Oxford University Press; a rough note-
book, kept by Isaac Milner, one of the most active
of the Cambridge Syndics, contains various memoranda concerning the Oxford method of management. Milner seems particularly to have discussed
with Mr Dawson, of the Clarendon Press, the proper
percentage of profit on the printing and selling of
bibles. One of Milner's notes is reproduced here as
being of interest not only in the history of Cambridge printing, but also in the history of business;

it should be added that there is a note appended to
the calculation explaining that "the 25 per cent.,
it is supposed, will nearly leave the proposed profit

An example of the manner of
Computing the Expences of
Manufact! & of selling.

Min. Bible.

1. A°. 10.000
2. taken 12.60 Reams of Paper = £1113..0.0
Printing. 4d - ___ 515.0.0
___ £1628.
add 25 ⅋C 407
20 3 5
Deduct. drawback
Plate or Paper ___ 147
1 8 8 8
Nominal price 4.6
retail D°. - 3.10¼ × 10000 = £1927
nominal price
at present sold for 3.6 :
old retail ___ 3. × 10000 = 1500

A PAGE FROM ISAAC MILNER'S NOTE-BOOK, 1800

of £10 per cent. and pay all the wear and tear and
salary of superintendence."

Richard Watts, the printer elected at Cambridge to succeed John Deighton in December, 1802, also appears to have had previous experience in Oxford, where he had conducted, and had a share in, a paper under Dr Manor, called the *Oxford Mercury*, in opposition to Dr Jackson's *Oxford Journal*. Immediately before his election he seems to have been agent for Mr Hamilton, a printer of Falcon Court, London.

A little more than a year after this appointment Cambridge received another offer of a secret for the process of stereotype printing. The inventor was the third Earl Stanhope, a remarkable man who, besides being prominent in political life, was a Fellow of the Royal Society, the author of *Principles of Electricity*, and the inventor of many devices including a microscopic lens, a new kind of cement, a calculating machine, an artificial tile for keeping out rain, a cure for wounds made in trees, an instrument for performing logical operations, and several improvements in the art of printing. Of these last the most important were the Stanhope press and an improved process of stereotyping: the Stanhope press was made of iron instead of wood and an ingenious mechanism made it possible to print a sheet twice as large as on the old wooden presses; the university bought two of these new presses, which are still in use at the present day.

The offer of the stereotype secret came to the university from Andrew Wilson, the London printer employed by Earl Stanhope. By a preliminary agreement of 20 April, 1804, Wilson was to receive for the space of 14 years one-third of the savings re-

sulting from the employment of the stereotype process and was to act, in conjunction with Watts, as
agent for the Syndics' bibles and prayer-books. The
savings were to be calculated by arbitrators appointed
by the respective parties.

This not very business-like arrangement naturally
led to a dispute before long. As early as October,
1805, Milner seems to have had misgivings both
about the scheme and about Wilson's competency,
as the following entries in his note-book show:

Qy whether Wilson's declaration of 30,000 profits in
8 years be not a proof want of judgm^t.

Qy whether Wilson be not an advent^r—without judgment.

Hints to new Vice-C^r.

1. The system of talking *before* them viz. Watts and
Wilson.

The absolute necessity of others being informed in the
stereotype art.

Watts talks of going to London again by Wilson's
directions to see what chases and things he wants—and
when I say he should not leave them, he says, Oh, there
is no more in leaving them now than when he was ill—
they are to be trusted.

Qy—Quid cogitant ille and Wilson.

Qy *x* to agree with Oxf^d? as a Stereotyper?

The supposition contained in the last cryptic note
was well justified, as Wilson had in March, 1805,
proposed to the Clarendon Press "to put the University in possession of the Art of Stereotype Printing"; later in the same year the Delegates, having
resolved that "the University of Cambridge being in
possession of the Art, it seems not only expedient,
but necessary, that Oxford should be possess'd of the

same advantages," entered into an agreement by which Wilson was to instruct their representatives in the stereotype processes for the sum of £4000[1].

In 1806 Wilson claimed that, as the introduction of stereotyping had enabled the Syndics to convert a warehouse into a printing-office for the sum of £1500 instead of building a new one at a cost of £4500, he was entitled by the agreement to his share of the saving of £3000 thus effected.

On 6 March, 1807, the university agreed to pay Wilson the sum of £865 16s 9d for the composition and two sets of plates of a bourgeois testament, a brevier testament and a nonpareil Welsh testament[2]; it being provided that the university should make for Wilson (from type supplied by himself) so many perfect plates towards octavo editions of Ainsworth's Dictionary and Johnson's Dictionary as should amount in value to the aggregate of Wilson's bill. Later in the same year the university definitely acquired the stereotype secret by a further agreement: £2000 was to be paid immediately, £1000 which had been previously advanced to Wilson was to become his property, and further sums were to be paid in accordance with the amount of the sales of bibles, testaments and prayer-books[3].

The following extracts, describing the outline of

1 *Collectanea*, vol. III, Part VII (*Oxford Historical Society*), where a full account (by Horace Hart) of Stanhope's invention and of his connection with the Clarendon Press will be found.

2 Details of Wilson's bill may be seen in Registry MS 33. 7. 24, and have been printed in Bowes, *Biographical Notes*, p. 327.

3 Registry MS 33. 7. 26.

the stereotype process, are taken from Milner's note-book:

1. The pages as they come from the composers have been first well cleansed with a solution of American Potash—14 lb in 3 buckets of water.

2. They must then be gently dried by the fire and then *cool* and a little oil of Turpentine is put on a plate with 2 parts sweet oil....This mixture gets thick by time: The plate is then well done over with a little of this mixture by one of the small soft brushes like a painter's brush....

3. Then a *copper measure* of the powdered calcined gypsum is taken—viz. about $\frac{1}{2}$ or $\frac{3}{4}$ pint and the same quantity of soft water and they are put into a copper vessel and shaken exceedingly well together: and then the mixture is to be poured upon the types, there being first placed upon them an iron frame to form an Edge to sustain the fluid Gypsum and water.

4. Immediately, and without the least loss of time the short square brushes are now to be taken and you must work the Air out quickly with them and continue working till the gypsum is too fixed to allow of more working.

5. When so fixed that you can easily make an impression, that is, while the Plaster is softish, take off the upper frame and scrape clean all the elevated plaster. It will rise again above the level by and by; scrape again—and lastly as soon as it is so fixed that it is not easy to make a mark with y^r nail, then lay it carefully upon a *soft frame* (covered with a sort of cloth) and then take a piece of wood that nearly fits the cake, and gently thrust it so as to make it quit the frame; and then dress it with a knife and lay it between two pieces of marble to keep it from warping.

6. The types must now be cleaned by picking out any bits of gypsum left in the Interstices...and lastly they must be brushed; and then done over again for a new mold.

7. The artist, Mr Austen, Engraver can dress and cure any little imperfection in the plates when cast.

8. The Gypsum requires about 2 hours for calcination; and is known to be right when you break the pieces, and see them moulded quite thro'—Matter of Experience.

9. The Gypsum should be broken with small bits about 2 ounces each.

10. and when calcined they are to be ground on a Stone....

11. When the moulds are made, and placed between the marbles...they will be ready in 2 or 3 hours for baking....

12. They are to be baked being placed upright on stands like those for toasted bread—raised a little from the bottom of the furnace—About 2 hours or $2\frac{1}{2}$ hours will take the moulds....

Casting

The metal is precisely the Type metal. The Pots must be made quite as hot as the metal—or rather more—Then the floating plate must be placed in the frame—and the cake or mould directly upon it with its face downwards: Then place upon the top the cover of the frame, and screw it down: and dip the whole in metal melted so that a match will light at it.—The melted metal will run in at those places made in the mould by the bits of brass —till all be full—and then remove the whole to be cooled on a tile in water with lime upon it—and as it cools and shrinks, supply with fresh melted metal.

The acquisition of this secret did not end the disputes with Wilson; the university in 1811 protested against payment of the bill referred to in the agreement of March, 1807, on the ground that Wilson had not supplied them with the type for Ainsworth's and Johnson's Dictionaries and that they were so prevented from selling the plates to him. No documents have been preserved to show how the case ended, but the following hypothetical case on which the university invited the opinion of counsel about this time may be quoted in conclusion:

Whether supposing A.B. to be acquainted with the secret mode of making stereotype plates, and supposing C.D. to know the mode now in general use, and whereas it is conceived that the secret is now no secret. Supposing A.B. to inquire of C.D. his (C.D.'s) mode of making the plates, and by his answers it appeared that he (C.D.) was acquainted with all the peculiarities of the secret, would A.B. be justified in telling C.D. that such was the secret?

Meanwhile, the Press buildings were growing. On the site of the White Lion Inn, bought in 1762, a warehouse had been built in 1786 and on 20 April, 1804, the Syndics instructed Mr Watts, with the assistance of Mr Humphreys, to "prepare a plan for altering the Warehouse into a Printing office." This building was described by Dyer, writing in 1809, as "a commodious brick building, situated in Silver Street, with a stereotype foundry adjoining" and, as has been already seen, it was claimed that this economical conversion was made possible by the introduction of stereotype printing.

The Syndics' relations with their printer at this time were not altogether happy. In 1808 two of the Syndics (Dr Milner and Mr Wood) were appointed to examine the Press accounts, since it was alleged that, in contrast to the average annual profit of £1 500 for a number of years before 1802, Watts had shown no profit at all for five years. These charges were set forth in a pamphlet entitled *Facts and Observations relative to the state of the University Press*, to which Watts wrote a *Reply*. Watts resigned as soon as the enquiry was instituted and, when the examination of the accounts was completed in the next year, it was decided to elect a new printer. Apart from the various stereotype editions of the bible and prayer-book no books of great importance seem to have been printed by Watts.

His successor, John Smith, was elected in 1809 and held the office of printer for 26 years.

It was during this period that the University Press began to assume its present appearance[1]. By 1820 the existing buildings had become quite inadequate to the growing business of the Press and the Syndics recommended the university to purchase Mr James Nutter's estate in Silver Street for the sum of £5060. The following grace was accordingly passed by the Senate on 24 January, 1821:

Quum in Typographeo vestro, ex angustiis loci, multa detrimenta atque incommoda subinde exoriri soleant; quumque, in remedium mali istius, Preli Typographici Curatores pactionem inierint cum Domino Nutter, ut facultate a vobis impetrata, quasdam domos illius quinque mille et sexaginta librarum pretio redimerunt: Placeat Vobis, ut pactio ista rata ac firma habeatur, atque ut summa praedicta e cista communi, usibus istis destinanda, erogetur.

The property thus acquired was on the site of the ancient inn known as The Cardinal's Cap. Its boun-

1 The provision of refreshment at meetings of the Syndicate had also been introduced by this time. A receipt for tea, coffee, muffins, and toast provided during the years 1815 and 1816 is preserved at the Press.

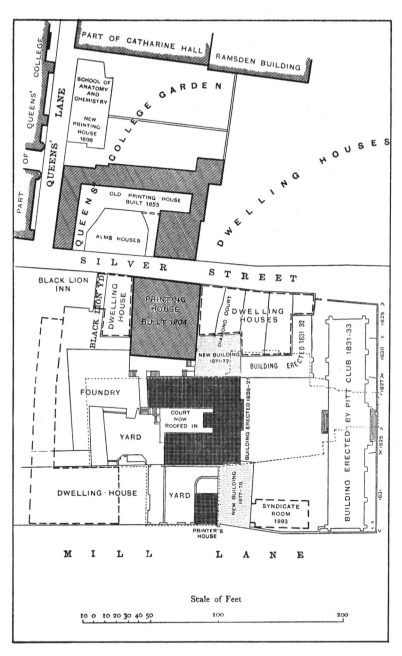

PLAN OF THE PRESS BUILDINGS
(Based on Willis & Clark, III. 132. Recent additions are marked ----)

daries are marked on the plan and in 1824, the Syndics of the Press, having taken the advice of an "eminent London Printer" (Mr Hansard), recommended that, as the existing buildings were "so dilapidated and so inadequate to the effectual conducting of the business," immediate steps should be taken towards extension. In the next year plans by James Walter for a new printing-house on the west side of the quadrangle and a printer's house in Mill Lane were approved by the Senate. These buildings were completed in January, 1827, the fitting of them being superintended by Thomas Hansard[1].

A more famous addition to the Press buildings is that associated with the name of William Pitt.

On 25 May, 1824, the following letter was addressed to the Vice-Chancellor (John Lamb, Master of Corpus Christi College) by the Marquess Camden, chairman of the London Pitt Club Committee:

Sir,

I have the Honor to inform you that I am just returned from a Meeting of the Committee appointed to consider of the disposal of the surplus of Money subscribed, many years ago, for the Erection of a Statue to the memory of Mr Pitt.

I am, now, authorized by that Committee to state to you, Sir, that which I had the Honor of personally communicating to you at Cambridge: 'the disposition of that Committee to recommend to a general Meeting of Subscribers to the Fund above-mentioned the Disposal of a considerable Sum of Money for the Erection of an handsome Building connected with the University Press at

---

1 In recognition of his services Hansard was presented by the Syndics with "a handsome silver inkstand with an appropriate inscription."

Cambridge;' but, as it will be necessary to state to the general Meeting how far the University is disposed to find and provide a proper Scite for the erecting such Building, near or opposite to Pembroke College, I now trouble you on that subject, and I request you will have the goodness to inform me how far I may be authorized to inform the General Meeting of the Disposition of the University to find and provide a proper Scite as above-mentioned for the erecting of an handsome Building, which the Committee is desirous should be erected on such a scale as to be a distinguished Ornament to the University, and tend to perpetuate the Name and Memory of Mr Pitt

I have the Honor to remain, Sir,
Your most obedient humble Servant,
CAMDEN.

A favourable reply having, no doubt, been received from the university, the Committee, at a meeting held at the Thatched House Tavern on 18 June, 1824, unanimously passed the following resolution:

That the surplus of the Fund, after defraying the Expense of the Statue in Hanover-Square, as resolved at the former meeting on the 11th instant, be applied to the Erection of a handsome and appropriate Building at Cambridge, connected with the University Press; such to bear the name of Mr Pitt. That the Committee be desired to take the necessary steps for carrying into execution this Resolution.

The university, on its part, appointed a Syndicate with authority to expend the sum of £8000 in purchasing "houses or leases of houses for the purpose of making exchanges with the Proprietors of the houses between Silver Street and Mill Lane fronting towards Trumpington Street."

After some years of delay the Committee approved

the designs submitted by Edmund Blore, who came to Cambridge with a letter of introduction from the Marquess Camden in 1829. In this letter the desire of the Committee for an imposing central chamber and staircase is evident:

It is necessary to premise, that the Committee is desirous that an handsome Room should be included in the Design, together with a staircase leading to it, but that the Committee would be most desirous any Accommodation could be given to the Press in the Building to be erected which did not interfere with those parts which they think should be ornamented.

Subsequently the university obtained the whole frontage between Mill Lane and Silver Street—a larger site than that on which Blore's original design had been based. Furthermore, the Pitt statue in Hanover Square cost more than had been anticipated. The Pitt Memorial Committee, therefore, undertook to erect the main building in Trumpington Street at a cost of £9000, while the university authorised an expenditure of not more than £2000 upon the buildings (also designed by Blore) which form the north side of the Press quadrangle.

The first stone of the Pitt Press building was laid by the Marquess Camden on 18 October, 1831, and the work was completed in about eighteen months, the total cost being £10,711 8s 9d.

It consists of three floors with a square central tower containing a lofty room designed for the Press Syndicate, but now used as the Registry of the University. As to the architectural style of the building, comment may best be confined to the repetition of Willis and Clark's laconic description: "The style of the building is Late Perpendicular." Some extracts from the account of the opening on 28 April, 1833, abridged from *The Cambridge Chronicle* (1 May, 1833), may also be given in conclusion:

The Pitt Press having been completed, Tuesday last was appointed for the Vice-Chancellor to receive the key of the building from the Marquis Camden and a deputation of the Pitt Committee....Having arrived at the building the Marquis Camden, accompanied by the members of the Committee, proceeded into the grand entrance hall, and having invited the Vice-Chancellor to the door, spoke as follows:

"Mr Vice-Chancellor and Gentlemen of the University of Cambridge: The idea of connecting the name of Mr Pitt with the Press of that University to which he owed his education and so much of his fame, was met by all parties with enthusiasm. The University have displayed an activity and liberality in providing this magnificent site which could only have been prompted by an admiration for the character of Mr Pitt. The Committee, animated by a personal respect and affection towards their contemporary, have endeavoured to cause to be erected on this site, such a building as might prove an addition to the other great improvements already perfected in this place and which, from its peculiar destination, will unite the name of Mr Pitt with all those works of religion, morality, and science, which will in future emanate from it, and diffuse throughout the world the connexion of his name with erudition and learning....

Sir, you have caused this ceremony to be attended by all the undergraduates as well as by the dignitaries of the University. Let me call the peculiar attention of all to this ceremony, and allow me to impress on the undergraduates that we, Mr Pitt's contemporaries, have been witnesses of his uniting the closest study with the utmost cheerfulness, and, when not employed in solving the most abstruse problems, he has engaged the admiration of his friends and companions, by the liveliest sallies of wit and imagination. Let his example stimulate you to the greatest exertion during your residence in this place, so well calculated to provide for your instruction in every department of literature and science."[1]

The key was then presented to the Vice-Chancellor, who grew eloquent in his reply:

What more appropriate monument then could be erected to the memory of Pitt than this building, the chief purpose and object of which is to send forth to the world the Word of God; and could he, with prophetic eye, when residing in yon neighbouring college, whose proudest boast is to number him among her sons—could he have beheld such a structure, bearing his name, raised for such a purpose, and erected by such friends, even his own eloquence would have scarce sufficed to express the feelings of his heart. My Lord, the edifice with which you have adorned this University, and the illustrious name it bears, will add a fresh stimulus to our exertions in the dissemination of truth, the extension of science, and the advancement of religious knowledge; and I humbly trust that nothing will ever issue from these walls but such works as may conduce to the furtherance of these important objects....[1]

After which, the company, having printed off copies of the inscription on the foundation-stone from a press specially set up for the occasion, "went upstairs into the Syndicate Room, where they partook of a cold collation given by the Press Syndicate."

In the early part of his career, John Smith laboured under the difficulties arising out of the "dilapidated and inadequate" condition of the old Press buildings. The chief source of business continued to be the sale of bibles and prayer-books and agencies were

[1] Quoted in Willis and Clark, III, 142.

arranged with Rivingtons, Baldwin & Co., and other London booksellers.

Of the books printed by Smith the most notable are the editions of classical authors for which the "Great Porson Greek" type was used. This fine fount had been cut under Porson's direction by Austin, of London, with the assistance of Richard Watts and was used for various editions of the Greek tragedians by Blomfield, Monk, and Scholefield.

In 1824 the King expressed his gracious pleasure that the newly discovered MS of Milton should be printed at the University Press and a new fount of pica type (weighing 12 cwt.) was specially ordered from Messrs Millar, of Edinburgh, for the purpose[1].

In 1827 the Syndics, having again taken counsel of eminent London printers and booksellers (Charles and John Rivington, Mawman, Baldwin, Hansard, Gilbert), resolved upon the expediency of appointing "a Superintendent of the concerns of the Press in all its departments, immediately under the Vice-Chancellor and General Syndicate," and, while no charges were brought against the technical quality of Smith's printing, there seems to have been a general feeling that he was not adequate to the control of the whole business. Smith's *Observations relating to the Affairs of the Press* (16 March, 1829) throw an interesting light on the difficulties with which he had to contend. He begs to observe, for instance, that many of the works brought to the Press are in the most unprepared state possible...the consequence is, that

1 Syndics' Minute Book 1823–43, from which various extracts are quoted in the later part of this chapter.

when proof-sheets are sent to the respective Authors, the work is much cut-up, and subject to continued Over-runnings and Corrections.... The Authors, for the most part being Gentlemen of the University engaged with Pupils during Term-time, furnish their Copy in detail— loosely written—and frequent suspensions of MS, which necessarily occasions great delay and inconvenience.... The Gentlemen of the Press Syndicate must be aware (tho' a London Printer cannot, unless he witnessed the operation) that the Examination-Papers which of late years have abundantly increased, must from their nature have retarded all regular work in the Composing Room. These papers could only be executed by Workmen competent and accustomed to Mathematical and Greek Composition; and my best Mathematical Compositors are those who have been brought up and trained in our own Office: London Workmen having in several instances left the Office, rather than undertake the Composition of such Works[1].

Smith also claims a development of the bible business:

I had the honour of being elected Printer at the close of 1809—at that time the number of Presses employed did not exceed eight: the number increased in 1812 and 1813 to thirteen. At this period, and on to 1815 and 17 increased and increasing Orders flowed in from the British and Foreign Bible Society and also (through Messrs Rivingtons) from the Society for Promoting Christian Knowledge....

The fact is, that from 1813 to 1815 the demand for Bibles etc was such, that had the same quantity of work to be executed been required to be finished in the manner in which the same books are now printed, they would not possibly have been done with the means the Press then possessed—"Send up the Books in gatherings" (i.e. divisions) was the repeated order of the Bible Society—

1 Registry MS 33. 1. 46.

"and we will spare you the trouble of booking off etc, etc." Many thousand copies were thus supplied which were never properly dried....

Finally, a statement is presented showing an average annual profit of £3191 from 1809 to 1827.

The Syndics, however, adhered to their view and invited Mr Clowes, of London, to examine the Press; Clowes sent his overseer, John William Parker, and in February, 1829, was appointed Superintendent of the Press at a salary of £400 a year on the understanding that, while he himself should execute the London business which the appointment involved, the actual superintendence at Cambridge should be deputed to Parker.

Parker infused new life into the business: he introduced improved methods of book-keeping, bought new types and hydraulic presses, installed an apparatus "for warming the Press buildings by means of heated air," and in 1832 established a depository for the sale of Cambridge bibles and prayer-books at his house in the Strand.

When John Smith retired with a pension in 1836, Parker was appointed printer in his place, visiting Cambridge for two days every fortnight; the bible business continued to expand and in 1838 Parker could offer fifty-six different editions of the bible and prayer-book. One bible calls for special comment: on 10 January, 1835, King William IV wrote to the Marquess Camden from the Pavilion, Brighton, suggesting that there should be printed at Cambridge, as at Oxford, a certain number of bibles for presentation to sovereigns visiting the country. The

Chancellor conveyed the suggestion to the Syndics who unanimously agreed "that in obedience to His Majesty's command a quarto Bible with marginal references be immediately put to press"; 250 copies, printed on Imperial paper, were to be reserved for purposes of presentation and one copy was to be struck off on vellum for the King himself; larger editions were to be printed on ordinary paper for general sale and Parker was instructed to order a special fount of English type.

Reductions in the cost of bibles were also effected and the Royal Commission of 1850–52 remarked upon the great reduction of price between 1830 and 1850 "attributable to improved machinery and to better arrangements in the establishment." One of the most important of these improvements was the introduction of steam-power for printing, the Syndics resolving on 13 June, 1838, "that it appears expedient to introduce machinery into the Pitt Press." For many years, however, the Bible Society stoutly refused to purchase books printed by steam presses.

Apart from the great advances made in the actual processes of printing during this period, Parker's work is also of great importance in the development of Cambridge publishing.

As has been already noted, Parker established a publishing house in the Strand in 1832 and besides acting as agent for Cambridge bibles, he included in his catalogue the greater part of the educational books printed at the Press. The stock-books kept at Cambridge show that the bulk of the editions were delivered to Parker's warehouse in London or to

Deighton's in Cambridge and the names of both firms frequently appear on title-pages. University publications, together with classical, mathematical, and theological text-books and treatises, predominate in the list and the names of such scholars as Blomfield, Babington, Colenso, Donaldson, Hare, Monk, Paley, Scholefield, Shilleto, Trench, and Whewell are to be found amongst the authors.

In 1844 it was proposed to reprint a number of standard works in theology and general literature "in order to provide against the loss which the want of full employment for the Workmen frequently occasions." It was hoped that by such an undertaking "the University would not only be enabled to secure regular occupation for their Printing Establishment, but would, also, acquire a copyright-interest in certain important Works which would ultimately prove a permanent source of income." Out of a long list three titles were chosen for publication: Stillingfleet's *Conferences and Tracts*, Cosin's *History of the Canon*, and Knight's *Life of Erasmus*.

Not all the books printed, of course, can be regarded as the publications of the Syndics of the Press. Some were printed to the order of an author or bookseller or society (e.g. the Parker Society); others were private ventures of Parker himself (such as his series of *Popular Literature* including *Linnaeus and Botany*, *Smeeton on Lighthouses*, *Cuvier and Natural History*, *Sir Joseph Banks and the Royal Society*); but others were definitely the property of the university, as the following minute of the Syndics of 25 May, 1838, shows:

At a meeting of the Syndicate held this day it was agreed, that the following be the form of an imprint for the New Edition of Wilson's Illustrations etc of the New Testament and that the same be adopted as the imprint in all such editions of books as shall be retained as the property of the University

Cambridge, printed at the Pitt Press,

by J. W. Parker, Printer to the University

and again in 1850 it was ordered that it should be stated on the title-page whether the book was printed for the author, editor, or publisher.

Towards the end of Parker's career in Cambridge, there was a distinct decline of business; the extension of the right of printing bibles to the Scottish printers in 1842 led to "the forced production of inferior editions which gradually lowered the prices of those of better quality produced in England." The Syndics, in a report to the Senate in 1849, while declaring the management of the previous 20 years to have been most satisfactory, found themselves faced by two alternatives for the future: either a large outlay upon new types and stereotype plates, or the placing of the establishment upon a reduced footing—and the second course was recommended.

The condition and extent of the Press in 1852 is summarised in the statement prepared by the Syndics for the Royal Commission.

There were at this time eighteen Syndics, who met once a fortnight during term; by a grace of 1752 five (of whom one must be the Vice-Chancellor or his deputy) constituted a quorum and the average attendance was $7\frac{9}{23}$.

The printing-office contained frames for 70 compositors, presses for 56 press men, and 8 printing machines, requiring about 50 men and boys to work them; a 10-horse steam-engine, 2 boilers, twining lathe, forge, and circular saw; one steam power milling machine, hydraulic and screw hot presses employing about 100 men and boys in all. The machinery was claimed to be "good of its kind." There was provision also for "any number of Readers, Observers, Warehousemen and Boys, necessary to carry on, get up, complete, and deliver the greatest amount of work which could at any time be done."

The two financial privileges enjoyed by the Press were the 'drawback' of $1\frac{1}{2}d$ a lb. on the paper duty and the Government annuity of £500, less income tax[1].

The business of the Press was defined as consisting of the printing of bibles, testaments, and prayer-books; of printing work for the university and colleges; of printing books edited for the Syndics; of book and job printing for the members of the university; of printing works published by the Parker and other learned societies; and of "such Book work, as, subject to the 'Imprimatur' of the Vice-Chancellor, may be offered by Publishers and other connexions of the Press."

Finally, the Syndics declared that it did not appear to them that any change of management could produce greater profits than were at that time realised.

Parker retired in 1854 and, in spite of the serious fluctuations in the bible trade, the first half of the

1 See pp. 100, 115.

nineteenth century must be regarded as a period of
expansion in building, in machinery, and in business.
For the first time the chief servant of the Syndics
was a man with an intimate knowledge of the book
trade, who served the university as publisher as well
as printer. The assumption by the Syndics themselves
of the full responsibilities of a publishing firm was
reserved for the later half of the century.

VIII

THE LATEST AGE

IN spite of the statement of the Syndics quoted at the end of the preceding chapter, the University Commissioners of 1850–52 reported their opinion that

it is only by associating printers or publishers in some species of co-partnership with the University, or by leasing the Press to them, that any considerable return can hereafter be expected from the capital which has been invested in it...we are satisfied that no Syndicate, however active and well chosen, can replace the intelligent and vigilant superintendence of those whose fortune in life is dependent upon its success.

Accordingly, on the resignation of Parker, the Syndicate recommended that the university should enter into partnership with "Mr George Seeley of Fleet Street, London, Bookseller, and Mr Charles John Clay, M.A. of Trinity College and of Bread Street Hill, London, Printer," and the grace for the deed of partnership was passed on 3 July, 1854.

The control of the printing thus came into the hands of Mr Clay, whilst Mr Seeley received the sole agency for the sale of Cambridge bibles and prayer-books; Mr Seeley, however, retired two years later and Mr Clay entered into a fresh agreement with the university.

The period of Mr Clay's management was one of great expansion. At the end of his first ten years of office it was estimated that the Press produced about four or five times as much as when he first undertook the management; in 1876, and again in 1886, the Syndics reported to the Senate that the business had attained a considerable magnitude and that large additions had been made to the machinery and plant.

Increase of business naturally demanded increased accommodation and in 1863 a foundry was built upon the site of some old cottages in Black Lion Yard. Eight years later new machine-rooms and warehouses were built on the site of Diamond Court, leading out of Silver Street, and a still larger addition was made in 1877-78, when a three-storied building was erected in the south-west corner of the quadrangle. The most recent additions are the extensions of the warehouse and machine-room on the Silver Street side and the red brick building (containing the syndicate room and secretarial offices), which forms the south side of the quadrangle[1].

In 1882 Mr John Clay, son of Mr C. J. Clay, was admitted into the partnership with the university and from 1886 to 1904 Mr C. F. Clay was also associated with it. Mr John Clay became university printer on his father's retirement in 1895 and held the office until his death in 1916, when the partnership was dissolved and the present printer, Mr J. B. Peace, Fellow of Emmanuel College, was appointed. From 1917 to 1919 the Syndics also employed the services of Mr Bruce Rogers, whose distinguished work as a printer is well known on both sides of the Atlantic. One of the best known figures in the Press in the later half of the nineteenth century was that of Alfred Mason. His remarkable personality

1 See plan, facing p. 128.

dominated the counting-house for a long period and when he died in 1919 he had been for 65 years in the service of the Press.

The present buildings of the Press include machine-rooms, containing large quad royal and quad demy perfectors, revolution presses, and single cylinder machines; a foundry comprising a stereotyping department, an electro-moulding room, an electro-battery room, and two finishing rooms; type store-rooms, composing-rooms, and monotype-rooms; an art department for lithographic, half-tone, and other process work; and the warehouse, where the finished sheets are stored ready to be sent away for binding. Every month an average of 40 tons of printed matter leaves the Press to be delivered to London binders.

Printing is done in a wide variety of languages, including Hebrew, Arabic, Pali, Coptic, Sanskrit, Hausa, Syriac and Amharic, and the type catalogue makes a volume of about 200 pages.

Perhaps the greatest fame of the Cambridge Press rests upon its mathematical typography. To glance at a page, say, of *Principia Mathematica* is to realise a little—but only a little—of the minute care and skill required of the compositor, the press-reader, and the machine-minder in the production of such a book. It may be permissible here, perhaps, to quote one recent tribute from the preface to Professor E. W. Brown's *Tables of the Motion of the Moon*, printed in 1918 for the Yale University Press:

The reading of the proof has been almost entirely directed to the detection of errors in the manuscript.

That this has been possible is due to the remarkable record of the Cambridge University Press which in setting up over five hundred quarto pages of numerical tables has allowed less than a dozen printer's errors to pass its proof-readers and has, in addition, frequently queried our own mistakes. Few sheets have required a second proof and in the actual use of the Tables, as finally printed, for the calculation of the ephemeris for two years, no error of any kind has been detected.

On the retirement of Mr George Seeley in 1856, Messrs Hamilton, Adams & Co., of Paternoster Row, were appointed as agents for the Syndics' books[1]. This arrangement, however, does not seem to have been satisfactory, as the name of a new agent—George Cox—appears in the following year; a further change was made in 1862 when the firm of Rivingtons became agents for Cambridge books; finally, when this agreement came to an end, ten years later, the Syndics reported to the Senate that "acting on the advice of Mr Clay" they had decided "not to appoint other Agents, but to conduct their London business in an office of their own, under the superintendence of a paid Manager" and that they had agreed "to take a Lease of convenient premises in Paternoster Row."

The beginning of the Syndics' career as London publishers—in the strict sense of the term—must therefore be assigned to the year 1872. At that time the number of books published by the Syndics— apart from bibles and prayer-books—was very small. Among them, however, may be noted the first volume of Mullinger's *The University of Cambridge*,

1 The catalogue of *Works edited for the Syndics* (1857) contained about 25 titles.

published in 1873, the first instalment of a monumental work which remained uncompleted at the author's death in 1917.

In 1874 an important step was taken, the Syndics deciding to publish a series of editions of Greek, Latin, French, and German authors designed for use in schools and especially for candidates for the Local Examinations. This was the beginning of the Pitt Press Series, which now includes over 300 volumes, and such editions as Sidgwick's *Virgil* and Mr Verity's *Shakespeare*—to name but two out of many—have become familiar to many generations of schoolboys.

The Syndics' catalogue for 1875 (a pamphlet of 16 tiny pages) reflects the beginnings of schoolbook publishing: it opens with some nine volumes in the Pitt Press Series; then follow Scrivener's *Paragraph Bible*, Scholefield's *Greek Testament* and several theological works including Isaac Barrow's *Works* in nine volumes; there are five editions of Greek and Latin authors, among them being Paley and Sandys's *Private Orations of Demosthenes* and Heitland's *Cicero pro Murena*; mathematics and physics claim nine books, including Kelvin and Tait's *Elements of Natural Philosophy*; history is represented by Mullinger's first volume, already referred to, and Mayor's edition of Baker's *History of St John's College*; of law books there are three, including Whewell's edition of *Grotius de Iure Belli ac Pacis*; and the list ends with a few catalogues and university examination papers.

In 1877 the publication of another important series was begun—*The Cambridge Bible for Schools*. The general editor was Dr J. J. S. Perowne, afterwards Bishop of Worcester, and the first volume to appear was Maclear's *St Mark*.

Originally designed for school use, the series soon attained a wider public. It was begun before the publication of the Revised Version and at the very time when the controversy was raging in Scotland which resulted in the suspension of Robertson Smith from his professorship at Aberdeen; when the series was finally completed by Sir George Adam Smith's *Deuteronomy* in 1918, many of the older volumes had already been replaced or revised. On the death of Bishop Perowne in 1904 *The Times* referred to the series as one which had "done more to spread accurate Biblical knowledge among English-speaking people than any book except the Revised Version."

The agreements between the university presses and the two companies of revisers for the publication of the Revised Version had been completed, "after much careful consideration as well as protracted negotiation," in 1873.

Three years earlier the New Testament company had held the first of its 407 meetings in the Jerusalem Chamber of Westminster Abbey. The company included the most distinguished theologians of the time —Hort, Westcott, Lightfoot, Ellicott, Scrivener, W. F. Moulton—and at first an average of only seventeen verses was revised in the daily session. Later, however, progress became a little more rapid and the revision was completed on 11 November, 1880. The Revised New Testament was published jointly by the university presses in 1881 and the Old

Testament three years later. The secretary of the Old Testament company was W. Aldis Wright, for more than 30 years a Syndic of the Cambridge Press.

By 1890 the catalogue of the Syndics' publications had grown considerably, not only by additions to the Pitt Press and other Series, but by the publication of larger works on literary and scientific subjects, such as Robertson Smith's *Kinship and Marriage in early Arabia*, Willis and Clark's *Architectural History of the University of Cambridge*, Maitland's edition of *Bracton's Note Book*, and Jebb's *Sophocles*.

Cayley's *Collected Mathematical Papers*, in thirteen volumes, were published between 1889 and 1897, and have since been followed by similar collections of the mathematical and scientific work of Kelvin, Rayleigh, Reynolds, Stokes, Sylvester, Tait, and other scholars. Meanwhile, larger publishing premises were found to be necessary, and in 1884 the London office was moved to Ave Maria Lane; with the growth of business these premises similarly became inadequate and the lease of the present offices in Fetter Lane was bought by the university in 1904.

One of the most important of the Syndics' undertakings towards the end of the last century was *The Cambridge Modern History*. Lord Acton had been elected Regius Professor of Modern History in 1895 and early in 1896 the Syndics approached him with a view to the compilation of a great English universal history. In his report of 15 July, 1896 Lord Acton wrote:

Universal history is not the sum of all particular histories, and ought to be contemplated, first, in its distinctive essence, as Renaissance, Reformation, Religious Wars, Absolute Monarchy, Revolution, etc. The several countries may or may not contribute to feed the main stream, and the distribution of matter must be made accordingly. The history of nations that are off the line must not suffer; it must be told as accurately as if the whole was divided into annals....

and later in a more detailed report:

It will be necessary to prescribe exact limits and conditions, and to explain clearly what we desire to obtain, and to avoid. We shall avoid the needless utterance of opinion, and the service of a cause. Contributors will understand that we are established not under the meridian of Greenwich, but in longitude 30 West; that our Waterloo must be one that satisfies French and English, Germans and Dutch alike....Ultimate history we cannot have in this generation; but we can dispose of conventional history and show the point we have reached on the road from the one to the other....If History is often called the teacher and the guide that regulates public life, which, to individuals as to societies, is as important as private, this is the time and the place to prove the title....

The essential elements of the plan I propose for consideration are these:

Division of subjects among many specially qualified writers.

Highest pitch of knowledge without the display.

Distinction between the organic unity of general history and the sum of national histories, as the principle for selecting and distributing matter.

Proportion between historic thought and historic fact.

Chart and compass for the coming century.

Lord Acton, however, did not live to carry out the work and the editorship was entrusted to Sir A. W. Ward, Sir G. W. Prothero, and Sir Stanley Leathes.

The first of the volumes of text appeared in 1902 and the whole work was completed by a general index published in 1912.

This plan of co-operative history has been adopted by the Syndics in several other branches of learning: *The Cambridge History of English Literature* was completed under the editorship of Sir A. W. Ward and Mr A. R. Waller in 1916, and other works in progress are *The Cambridge Medieval History*, *The Cambridge History of India*, *The Cambridge History of British Foreign Policy*, and *The Cambridge Ancient History*.

Another important undertaking was the publication of the eleventh edition of the *Encyclopaedia Britannica* in 1911.

Short of summarising the forty-five main subject-headings of the current catalogue, it would be difficult —as well as invidious—to enter into further detail concerning the modern publications of the Cambridge University Press. It may suffice to note that in the years immediately preceding the war the average annual output of new books, exclusive of journals, was 150. This figure excludes, of course, the various editions of Cambridge bibles and prayer-books: at the present time there are, apart from the various styles of binding, 26 different editions of the Authorised, and 19 of the Revised Version; 19 editions of the English, and 6 of the Scottish prayer-book; of the latter, as of the new Canadian prayer-book, the Syndics are the sole publishers.

During the war both the printing and publishing

businesses suffered from shortage of personnel, of metal, and of paper. Two hundred and fifty-two servants of the Syndics joined His Majesty's forces and of these forty-one were killed, or died, on service.

In conclusion, it may be remarked that the method of the government of the Press by a body of Syndics appointed by the Senate of the university has, with certain important modifications, persisted since 1698.

The constitution of the Syndicate has been more than once revised—notably in 1782 and 1855—and the length of a Syndic's tenure of office varied from time to time. The present body consists of the Vice-Chancellor (*ex officio*) and fourteen Syndics; the term of appointment is seven years and two Syndics retire each year. The first permanent secretary, Mr R. T. Wright, formerly Fellow of Christ's College, was appointed in 1892; on his retirement in 1911 he was succeeded by the present secretary, Mr A. R. Waller, of Peterhouse.

The Syndics employ a staff of about 280 in Cambridge and of 110, under the management of Mr C. F. Clay, at their publishing office in Fetter Lane; their current catalogue contains the titles of some 2500 books bearing the *imprimatur* of the university.

Such, in brief summary, is the measure of the development of Cambridge printing since John Siberch set up his press at the sign of the *Arma Regia* in 1521.

APPENDIX

I. UNIVERSITY PRINTERS, 1521–1921

The names of those who are not known to have printed
anything in Cambridge are underlined

1521.	John Siberch	He disappears after 1522
1534.	Nicholas Speryng	
	Garrett Godfrey	
	Segar Nicholson	
1539.	Nicholas Pilgrim	
1540.	Richard Noke	
1546.	Peter Sheres	
1577.	John Kingston	
1583.	Thomas Thomas, M.A.	d. 1588
1588.	John Legate	d. 1620
?	John Porter (before 1593)	
1606.	Cantrell Legge	d. 1625
?	Thomas Brooke, M.A. (before 1608)	
		Resigned (?) 1625
1622.	Leonard Greene	d. 1630
1625.	Thomas Buck, M.A	At least till 1668
	John Buck, M.A.	At least till 1668
1630.	Francis Buck	Resigned 1632
1632.	Roger Daniel	Patent cancelled 1650
1650.	John Legate (*the younger*)	Patent cancelled 1655
1655.	John Field	d. 1668
1669.	Matthew Whinn	
1669.	John Hayes	d. 1705
1680.	John Peck, M.A.	
1682.	Hugh Martin, M.A.	
1683.	James Jackson, M.D.	
1683.	Jonathan Pindar	
1693.	H. Jenkes	

1697.	JONATHAN PINDAR	At least till 1730
1705.	CORNELIUS CROWNFIELD	Pensioned 1740
1730.	WILLIAM FENNER	
	MARY FENNER	Lease relinquished by Mrs Fenner
	THOMAS JAMES	1738
	JOHN JAMES	
1740.	JOSEPH BENTHAM	Resigned 1766
1758.	JOHN BASKERVILLE	Nothing after 1763
1766.	JOHN ARCHDEACON	D. 1795
1793.	JOHN BURGES	D. 1802
1802.	JOHN DEIGHTON	Resigned 1802
1802.	RICHARD WATTS	Resigned 1809
[1804.	ANDREW WILSON	(?) 1811]
1809.	JOHN SMITH	Pensioned 1836
1836.	JOHN WILLIAM PARKER	Resigned 1854
1854.	GEORGE SEELEY	Retired 1856
1854.	CHARLES JOHN CLAY, M.A.	Retired 1895
1882.	JOHN CLAY, M.A.	D. 1916
1886.	CHARLES FELIX CLAY, M.A.	Retired 1904
1916.	JAMES BENNET PEACE, M.A.	

II. CAMBRIDGE BOOKS, 1521–1750

The list of books from 1521 to 1650 is reprinted, with some additions, from that compiled by Mr F. Jenkinson and included in Bowes's *Catalogue of Cambridge Books*

There is some doubt about the books printed in italics

1521

Bullock (Hen.). Oratio. 4⁰.
Augustinus de miseria vitae. 4⁰.
Lucianus περὶ διψάδων. Bullock. 4⁰.
Balduinus de Altaris sacramento. 4⁰.
Erasmus de conscribendis epistolis. 4⁰.
Galenus de Temperamentis. Linacre. 4⁰.
Fisher (Joan.). Contio. Latin by R. Pace. 4⁰.

1522

Geminus (Papyrius). Hermathena. 4⁰.

Date not known (J. Siberch)

[Lily, Wm.]. De octo orationis partium constructione libellus. 4°.

1584

Bright (Tim.). In physicam G. A. Scribonii animadversiones. 8°.
Martinus (Jac.). De prima corporum generatione. 8°.
Ovidius. Fabularum interpretatio a G. Sabino. [Ed. T. T.]
Ramus (Petr.). Dialecticae libri duo, scholiis G. Tempelli. 8°.
Rouspeau (Yves) and J. de l'Espine. Two Treatises, translated. 8°.
Sadeel (Ant.). [La Roche de Chandieu (Ant.).] Disputationes. 4°.
[Stokes (M.).] Catalogus Rectorum et Cancellariorum.

1585

Pilkington (Jas.) and Rob. Some. Exposition on Nehemiah etc. 4°.
       "   "   Two treatises on Oppression. 8°.
Ramus (P.). Latin Grammar, in English. 8°.
[Stokes (M.).] Catalogus procancellariorum.
Ursinus (Zach.). Doctrinae christianae compendium. 8°.
Whitaker (W.). Answer to a book by W. Rainolds. 8°.
Willet (Andr.). De animae natura et viribus. 8°.

1586

Clarke (Wm.). Treatise against the Defense of the Censure. 8°.
Harmony of Confessions. 8°.

1587

Carmichael (Jas.). Grammaticae Latinae liber II. 4°.
Plato. Menexenus. 4°.
Thomas (Tho.). Dictionarium linguae Latinae. 8°.
Ursinus (Zach.). Explicationes catecheticae. Ed. 2. 8°.

1588

Whitaker (W.). Disputatio de sacra scriptura. 4°.

Sine anno (J. Legate)

Achilles Tatius. De Clitophontis et Leucippes amoribus. 8°.
Bastingius (J.). Exposition upon the Catechism. 8°.
Beza (T.). Job expounded. 8°.
      "   Ecclesiastes. 8°.
New Testament. (Genevan Version.) 24°. [Cotton gives 1589.]
Willet (Andr.). Sacrorum emblematum centuria una. 4°.

1589

Bastingius (J.). Exposition upon the catechism. 4°.
Cicero. De oratore libri tres. 16°.
Terentius. Comoediae sex. 12°.
Thomas (Tho.). Dictionarium linguae Latinae. Ed. 2. 8°.

1590

Greenwood (John). Syntaxis et prosodia. 8°.
Holland (Hen.). Treatise against Witchcraft. 4°.
Perkins (Wm.). Armilla Aurea. Edd. 1 and 2. 8°.
Willet (Andr.). De generali Judaeorum vocatione. 4°.

1591

Bible (Genevan version). 8⁰.
Perkins (W.). A Golden Chaine. 8⁰.

1592

L'Espine (Jean de). A very excellent Discourse (trs. by E. Smyth). 4⁰.
Lipsius (Justus). Tractatus ad historiam Romanam. 8⁰.
Perkins (W.). Prophetica. Ed. 2. 8⁰.
„   Armilla Aurea. Ed. 3 (n.d.).
„   A Golden Chaine. Ed. 2. 8⁰.
Sohn (Georg). A briefe and learned Treatise (trs. by N. G.). 8⁰.
Thomas (Tho.). Dictionarium. Ed. 3. 4⁰.
Zanchius (H.). Spirituall mariage. 16⁰.

1593

Bell (Thomas). T. Bels Motives. 4⁰.
[Cowell (John).] Antisanderus. Edd. 1 and 2. 4⁰.
Lysias. Eratosthenes, praelectionibus illustrata A. Dunaei. 8⁰.
More (John). Table from the beginning of the world. 8⁰.
Perkins (W.). Direction for the government of the tongue. 8⁰.
„   Two Treatises. 8⁰.

1594

Danaeus (Lamb.). Commentarie upon the twelve small Prophets. 4⁰.
G[reaves] (P.). Grammatica anglicana. 8⁰.
Hawenreuter (J. L.). Σύνοψις τῆς φυσικῆς τοῦ Ἀριστοτέλους. 8⁰.
The Death of Usury. 4⁰.
Thomas (Tho.). Dictionarium. Ed. 4. 8⁰.
Whitaker (W.). Adv. T. Stapletoni defensionem duplicatio. F⁰.

1595

Bastingius (J.). Exposition of the [Heidelberg] Catechism. 8⁰.
C. (W.). Polimanteia. 4⁰.
Lycophron. Ἀλεξάνδρα. 12⁰.
Perkins (W.). Two Treatises. 4⁰.
„   Two Treatises. Ed. 2. 8⁰.
„   Exposition of the Creed. 4⁰.
„   A Salve for a Sicke man. 8⁰.
„   A Golden Chaine (trs. by R. H.) Ed. 2. 4⁰.
„   A Direction for the government of the Tongue. 4⁰.
Plutarchus. Περὶ τοῦ ἀκούειν. 8⁰.
R[acster] (John). De hypocritis vitandis. 4⁰.

1596

G. (C.). A Watchworde for Warre. 4⁰.
Perkins (W.). Exposition of the Creed. Ed. 2. 4⁰.
Some (R.). Three questions. 8⁰.
The Apocalypse with exposition by F. Du Jon [trs. by T. B.]. 4ᶜ.
Thomas (Tho.). Dictionarium. Ed. 5. 4⁰.

1597

Pacius (Julius). Institutiones Logicae. 18⁰.
Perkins (W.). A Reformed Catholike (159).

Perkins (W.). A Golden Chaine. Ed. 2. 4⁰.
    ,,   Exposition of the Creede. 8⁰.
    ,,   Salve for a Sicke man (and other tracts). 4⁰. Edd. 1 and 2.
Praecepta in monte Sinai data. (Latine) per Ph. Ferd. Polonum. 4⁰.
Spiritual epistles. 4⁰.

1598

Bird (S.). Lectures upon Hebrews XI and Psalm XXXVIII. 8⁰.
    ,,   Lectures upon II Cor. VIII and IX. 8⁰.
Chemnitius (Mart.). Exposition of the Lords Prayer. 8⁰.
F[letcher]., I. Causes of urine. 8⁰.
Lincoln. Visitation Articles in the xl. yeare of Elizabeth. 4⁰.
Perkins (W.). De Praedestinationis modo. 8⁰.
    ,,   A Reformed Catholike. 8⁰.
Specimen Digesti sive Harmoniae etc. [by W. Perkins]. F⁰.
Stoughton (Tho.). General Treatise against Popery. 8⁰.
Terence in English, by R. B[ernard]. 4⁰.
Wilcox (Tho.). Discourse touching the Doctrine of Doubting. 8⁰.

1599

Dillingham (Fra.). A Disswasive from Poperie. 8⁰.
Polanus (Amandus). Treatise concerning Predestination. 8⁰.
Whitaker (W.). Praelectiones. + Cygnea Cantio. 4⁰.
Zanchius (Hieron.). Confession of Christian religion. 8⁰.

1600

Perkins (W.). A Golden Chaine (and 10 other works). 4⁰.
    ,,   A Treatise tending. 12⁰.
Thomas (T.). Dictionarium. Ed. 6. 8⁰.
Whitaker (W.). Praelectiones de conciliis. 8⁰.
    ,,   Tractatus de peccato originali. 8⁰.

1601

An Ease for Overseers of the Poor. 4⁰.
Hill (Rob.). Life everlasting. 4⁰.
Perkins (W.). How to live and that well. 12⁰.
    ,,   A warning against the Idolatry etc. 8⁰. (2 eds.)
[,,   ] The True Gaine. 8⁰.
    ,,   Foundation of Christian religion. 8⁰.

1602

Cogan (Tho.). Epistolarum Ciceronis epitome. 8⁰.
Dillingham (Fra.). Disputatio adv. R. Bellarminum. 8⁰.
Pagit (Eusebius). The Historie of the Bible. 12⁰.
[Perkins (W.).] Treatise of Gods free grace and mans free will. 8⁰.
Willet (A.). A Catholicon on Jude. 8⁰.

1603

Dillingham (Fra.). A Quartron of reasons prooved a quartron of follies. 4⁰.
    ,,   Tractatus in quo ex Papistarum confessione etc. 8⁰.
Heydon (Sir Christ.). Defence of Judiciall Astrologie. 4⁰.
James I. A Princes Looking Glasse (trs. by W. Willymot). 4⁰.

Perkins (W.). Works in one volume. F⁰.
,,   A Direction for the Tongue. 12⁰.
,,   A Treatise of Vocations. 8⁰.
,,   *A Treatise of Christian Equitie.*
,,   *The True Lawe of Free Monarchies.* 12⁰.
Playfere (Tho.). Power of praier. 8⁰.
,,   Heart's delight. 8⁰.
Sharpe (Leonell). Sermon before the University, 28 March. 8⁰.
,,   Dialogus inter Angliam et Scotiam. 8⁰.
Smith (J.). The bright morning star.
Sorrowes Joy. 4⁰.
Threnothriambeuticon. 4⁰.
Willet (A.). Ecclesia triumphans. 8⁰.

1604

Bownde (Nich.). The Holy Exercise of Fasting. 8⁰.
Gibbon (Cha.). The Order of Equalitie. 4⁰.
Manning (Jas.). A New Booke intituled I am for you all. 4⁰.
Oliver (Tho.). De sophismatum praestigiis cavendis. 4⁰.
Perkins (W.). Problema de Romanae fidei ementito catholicismo. 4⁰.
,,   Commentarie on Galatians. 4⁰.
,,   First Part of the Cases of Conscience. 8⁰.

1605

Bell (Thomas). T. Bels Motives. Ed. 2. 4⁰.
Cowell (John). Institutiones juris Anglicani. 8⁰.
Dillingham (Fra.). Spicilegium de Antichristo. 8⁰.
,,   Sermon. 8⁰.
In homines nefarios. (Gunpowder Plot.) 4⁰.
Leech (J.). Plaine and Profitable Catechisme for Householders. 8⁰.
Perkins (W.). Works. Vol. 1. F⁰.
Playfere (Tho.). The Sick Man's Couch. 8⁰.
Willet (A.). Hexapla in Genesin. F⁰.

1606

A Supplication of the Family of Love examined. 4⁰.
Dillingham (Fra.). Disputatio de natura Poenitentiae. 8⁰.
,,   Progresse in Pietie. 8⁰.
Hieron (Sam.). Truths Purchase. 8⁰.
Perkins (W.). Cases of Conscience. 8⁰.
Thomas (T.). Dictionarium. Ed. 7. 4⁰.

1607

Bernard (R.). A Double Catechisme. 8⁰.
,,   Terence. Ed. 2. 4⁰.
Cowell (John). The Interpreter. 4⁰.
Hieron (Sam.). Three Sermons. 4⁰.
,,   The Dignity of the Scripture. 4⁰.
Lipsius (Just.). Tractatus ad historiam Rom. cognoscendam. 8⁰.
Perkins (W.). A Treatise of Man's Imaginations. 12⁰.
[Rogers (Tho.).] The Faith of the Church of England. 4⁰.

Walsall (Sam.). Sermon before King at Royston. 4⁰.
Willet (A.). Loidoromastix. 4⁰.
  „   Harmonie upon Samuel I. 4⁰.

1608

Bownde (N.). The unbeleefe of S. Thomas the Apostle. 8⁰.
Hieron (S.). Sixe sermons. 4⁰.
Perkins (W.). A discourse of the damned art of witchcraft. 8⁰.
  „   *A treatise tending unto a declaration.* 12⁰.
  „   The whole treatise of the Cases of Conscience. 8⁰.
  „   A godly exposition of Christs Sermon in the Mount. 4⁰.
  „   Works. Vol. I. F⁰.
Walkington (T.). Salomons sweet harpe. 8⁰.

1609

Hieron (S.). Three sermons: A Remedie for securitie etc. 4⁰.
Perkins (W.). Works. Vol. II. Iohn Legat. F⁰.
  „   Works. Vol. III. Cantrell Legge. F⁰.
Playfere (T.). [Four Sermons.] 4⁰.

1610

Anthonie (Fr.). Medicinae, chymicae, et veri potabilis auri assertio, etc. 4⁰.
Ely Visitation Articles. 4⁰.
Fletcher (Giles). Christs Victorie. 4⁰.
Owen (D.). Herod and Pilate reconciled. 4⁰.
Perkins (W.). A discourse of the damned art of witchcraft. Ed. 2. 8⁰.
Playfere (T.). Ten sermons. 8⁰.
Thomas (T.). Dictionarium. Ed. 10. 8⁰.
Willet (A.). Hexapla in Danielem. F⁰.

1611

Perkins (W.). A godly exposition of Christs Sermon in the Mount. 4⁰.
Willet (A.). Hexapla upon Romans. F⁰.

1612

Cambridge University Act Verses.
Collins (S.). Increpatio Andreae Eudaemono-Johannis Jesuitae. 4⁰.
Epicedium Cantabrigiense. 2 eds. 4⁰.
Nethersole (Sir F.). Laudatio funebris. 4⁰.
Playfere (T.). Nine sermons. 8⁰.
Pownoll (N.). The young divines apologie. 8⁰.
Taylor (T.). Commentarie upon the epistle of Paul to Titus. 4⁰.
  „   Japhets first publique perswasion into Sems tents. 4⁰.

1613

Despotinus (Gaspar). Hirci Mulctra disceptatio medica. 4⁰.
Perkins (W.). Works. Vol. III. F⁰.
Robartes (Foulke). The Revenue of the Gospel is tythes. 4⁰.
S[mith] (S.). Art. Mag. Aditus ad Logicam.

1614

Kilby (R.). The Burthen. 8⁰.
Mosse (Miles). Justifying and Saving Faith distinguished. 4⁰.

Willet (Andr.). Harmonie upon the first booke of Samuel. F⁰.
    „   Harmonie upon the second booke of Samuel. F⁰.
    „   Ecclesia Triumphans. 3 pts. F⁰.

1615

God and the King, a dialogue. 8⁰.
Melanthe. Fabula Pastoralis. 4⁰. [By Mr Brookes.]
Yates (John). God's arraignment of Hypocrites. 4⁰.

1616

Farley (Henry). The Complaint of Paules to all Christian soules. 4⁰.
Gostwyke (Roger). The Anatomie of Ananias. 4⁰.
James I. Remonstrance for the Right of Kings. 4⁰.
Office of Christian parents. 4⁰.
Perkins (W.). Exposition of the Creede. 4⁰.
Stirbridge Fair Passes.
Yates (J.). God's arraignment.

1617

Collins (Sam.). Epphata to F. T. 4⁰.
Hieron (Sam.). David's Penitential Psalm opened in 30 several lectures. 4⁰.

1618

Perkins (W.). Works. Vol. III. F⁰.
Taylor (Tho.). Christ's Combate and Conquest. 4⁰.

1619

Angelos (Christopher). Ἐγκώμιον Μεγάλης Βρεττανίας. 4⁰.
    „   „   Ἐγχειρίδιον, Περὶ τῆς καταστάσεως τῶν Ἑλλήνων. 4⁰.
Gurnay (Edm.). Corpus Christi, a sermon. 12⁰.
James I. Remonstrance for the Right of Kings. 2 eds. 4⁰.
Lacrymae Cantabrigienses in obitum Annae. 4⁰.
Norwich Visitation Articles. 4⁰.
Sympson (W.). Full and profitable interpretation of proper names. 4⁰.
Taylor (Tho.). Commentarie upon the Epistle to Titus. 4⁰.

1620

Willet (Andr.). Hexapla upon Romans. F⁰.

1621

Playfere (Tho.). Nine Sermons. 8⁰.
Short Introduction of Grammar. 8⁰.

1622

Owen (David). Anti-Paraeus. 8⁰.

1623

Crakanthorpe (Ric.). De providentia Dei. 4⁰.
Gratulatio de S. P. reditu ex Hispaniis. 4⁰.
Herbert (G.). Oratio de Principis Caroli reditu ex Hispaniis. 4⁰.
The Whole Booke of Psalmes with apt notes to sing them. 8⁰.

1624

Chevalier (Guillaume de). The Ghosts of the deceased Sieurs de Villemor. 8⁰.

1625

Almanack. Sheet C. 8⁰.
Cantabrigiensium Dolor et Solamen. 4⁰.
    ,,   ,,   (with additions). 4⁰.
Epithalamium Caroli Regis et H. Mariae Reginae. 4⁰.
Novum Testamentum Graecum. 8⁰.

1626

Almanack (Strof). 8⁰.
Holland (Abr.). Hollandi Post-huma. 4⁰.
Sarpi (Paolo). Interdicti Veneti historia (trs. into Latin by W. Bedell). 4⁰.

1627

Almanacks (Dove, Frost, Lakes, Rivers, Strof, Waters). 8⁰.
Bishop's Book.
Davenant (Joh.). Expositio epistolae Pauli ad Colossenses. F⁰.
Fletcher (Phineas). Locustae. 4⁰.
Lincoln Visitation Articles. 4⁰.
Mede (Jos.). Clavis Apocalyptica. 4⁰.
Perrot (Rich.). Jacob's Vowe, or the true historie of Tithes. 4⁰.
Sudbury Visitation Articles. 4⁰.
Winterton (R.). Gerhard. Meditations. 12⁰.
Wren (Matth.). Sermon before the Kings Majestie. 4⁰.

1628

Bedell (Wm.). Examination of certaine motives to Recusansie. 8⁰.
Carter (John). Winter evenings communication with young novices. 8⁰.
Dent (Daniel). Sermon against drunkenness. 4⁰.
New Testament. 24⁰.
Sternhold (T.). Psalms in metre. 8⁰.
    ,,   ,,   12⁰.

1629

Almanacks (Pond, Rivers). 8⁰.
Bible. F⁰.
Common Prayer. F⁰.
Short Introduction of Grammar. 8⁰.
Sternhold (T.). Psalms in metre. F⁰.

1630

Bible. 𝕭. 𝕷. 4⁰.
   ,,   Roman Letter. 4⁰.
Cicero de officiis etc. 8⁰.
Common Prayer. 4⁰.
Davenant (John). Expositio epistolae ad Colossenses. 2nd ed. F⁰.
Lincoln Visitation Articles. 4⁰.
[Sarpi (Paolo).] Quaestio quodlibetica. [Trs. by W. Bedell.] 4⁰.
Sternhold (T.). Psalms in metre. 4⁰.

CAMBRIDGE BOOKS

1631

Aesopus. Fabulae. 8⁰.
Aphthonius. Progymnasmata. 8⁰.
Audomarus Talaeus. Rhetorica. 8⁰.
Castalio (Seb.). Dialogorum sacrorum libri IV. 8⁰.
Cicero. Epistolarum libri IV, a Jo. Sturmio. 8⁰.
Davenant (Jo.). Praelectiones. F⁰.
Genethliacum Caroli et Mariae. 4⁰.
Hippocratis aphorismorum liber primus, Gr. et Lat. 4⁰.
Moses Maimonides. Canones poenitentiae, Latine a G. N. 4⁰.
Ovidius. Metamorphosees. 12⁰.
Seton (J.). Dialectica. 8⁰.
Winterton (R.). Gerhard. Meditations. Ed. 2. 12⁰.

1632

Anthologia in Regis Exanthemata. 4⁰.
Baptista Mantuanus. Adolescentia. 8⁰.
Cruso (John). Militarie instructions for the Cavallerie. F⁰.
Dalechamp (Caleb). Christian Hospitalitie. Harrisonus honoratus. 4⁰
Fletcher (Giles). Christs Victorie. Ed. 2. 4⁰.
Heywood (Tho.). Englands Elisabeth. 12⁰.
Mede (Jos.). Clavis apocalyptica. Ed. 2. 4⁰.
Novum Testamentum, graece. 8⁰.
Randolph (Tho.). The Jealous Lovers. 4⁰.
Schonaeus (Corn.). Terentius Christianus. 8⁰.
Winterton (R.). Gerhard. A Golden Chaine. 12⁰.
　　　”　　　　”　Meditations. 12⁰.

1633

Bible. 𝕭. 𝕷. 4⁰.
Bible (2 states). 4⁰.
Castalio (Seb.). Dialogorum sacrorum libri IV. 8⁰.
Cicero, de Officiis. 12⁰.
Corderius (Matt.). Colloquiorum scholasticorum libri IIII. 8⁰.
Ducis Eboracensis fasciae a Musis Cantabrig. raptim contextae. 4⁰.
Fletcher (Giles). De literis antiquae Britanniae etc. 8⁰.
Fletcher (Phineas). The Purple Island, etc. 4⁰.
F[letcher] (P)[hineas]. Sylva Poetica. 8⁰.
Fosbrooke (Joh.). Six sermons. 4⁰.
Hausted (Peter). Senile Odium, comoedia. 8⁰.
Herbert (George). The Temple. 12⁰. (State A and State B.)
　　　”　　　　”　　　”　Ed. 2. 12⁰.
Hippocrates. Aphorismi, graece, + Epigrammata Reg. Med. Professorum. 8⁰.
Kellet (Edw.). Miscellanies of Divinitie. F⁰.
Nowell (Alex.). Christianae pietatis prima institutio. 8⁰.
Peterborough Visitation Articles. 𝕭. 𝕷. 4⁰.
Psalms with apt notes. 𝕭. 𝕷. 4⁰.
Rex redux. 4⁰.
Scot (Tho.). Assize Sermon at Bury St Edmunds. 4⁰.
Scott (J.). Broadsheet containing list of officers etc. Fragments.

R.　　　　　　11

Vives (Joan. Lud.). Linguae Latinae exercitatio. 8⁰.
Winterton (R.). Dionysius de situ orbis. 8⁰.

1634

Almanacks (Clark, Dove, Kidman, Rivers, Swallow, Turner, Winter). 8⁰.
Baptista Mantuanus. Adolescentia. 8⁰.
Cantebrigia (*Map*).
Crashaw (R.). Epigrammatum sacrorum liber. 8⁰.
Davenant (John). Determinationes quaestionum theologicarum. F⁰.
Donne (John). Six sermons. 4⁰.
Erasmus. Epitome colloquiorum. 8⁰.
Garthwaite (H.). Μονοτεσσαρον. The Evangelicall Harmonie. 4⁰.
Gerhard (John). Meditationes Sacrae. 24⁰.
Golius (Theophilus). Epitome doctrinae moralis ex decem libris Aristotelis. 8⁰.
Hawkins (Will.). Corolla varia. 8⁰.
Herbert (Geo.). The Temple. Ed. 3. 12⁰.
Lessius (Leonardus). Hygiasticon + Cornaro's Treatise. Edd. 1 and 2. 12⁰.
[Lily (Wm.).] A short introduction of Grammar. 8⁰.
Psalms. 4⁰.
Randolph (Thos.). The Jealous Lovers. 4⁰.
Russell (John). The two famous pitcht battles of Lypsich and Lutzen. 4⁰.

1635

Almanack. Broadsheet.
Anianus. Fabulae. 8⁰.
Aphthonius. Progymnasmata. 8⁰.
Audomarus Talaeus. Rhetorica. 12⁰.
Bible. 4⁰.
  ,,   𝕭. 𝕷. 4⁰.
Carmen natalitium ad cunas principis Elizabethae. 4⁰.
Common Prayer. 4⁰.
Cuique suum. ᾿Αντωδὴ contra Cathari cantilenam. 4⁰.
Dalechamp (Caleb). Haereseologia tripartita. 4⁰.
Erasmus. Epitome Colloquiorum. 12⁰.
Herbert (Geo.). The Temple. Ed. 4. 12⁰.
Hill, J. Schrevelius, Lexicon. 8⁰.
Kellet (Edw.). Miscellanies of Divinitie. F⁰.
Lincoln Visitation Articles. 4⁰.
Ovidius. Heroides, Amores, De arte amandi. 8⁰.
Ravisius (Joannes). Epistolae. 8⁰.
Schonaeus (Corn.). Terentius Christianus. 8⁰.
Shelford (Rob.). Five pious and learned discourses. 4⁰.
Swan (John). Speculum mundi. 4⁰.
Winterton (R.). Poetae minores Graeci. 8⁰.
  ,,   Gerhard. Meditations, Ed. 4 + Prayers, Ed. 5. 12⁰.

1636

Benlowes (Ed.). Sphinx Theologica. 8⁰.
Cade (Ant.). Sermon of the Ceremonies of the Church. Appendix. 4⁰.
Dalechamp (C.). Haeresologia Tripartita. 4⁰.
Dugres (Gabriel). Grammaticae Gallicae compendium. 8⁰.
Hodson (William). Credo resurrectionem carnis. Ed. 2. 12⁰.

Lessius (Leonardus). Hygiasticon. Ed. 3. 12⁰.
Manutius (Aldus). Phrases linguae Latinae. 8⁰.
[Nowell (Alex.).] Christianae pietatis prima institutio. 8⁰.
Saltmarsh (John). Poemata sacra, latine et anglice scripta. 8⁰.
Simson (Edw.). Mosaica. 4⁰.
Winterton (R.). Drexelius. Considerations upon Eternitie. 12⁰.

1637
Bible. (Colophon 1638.) 4⁰.
„ 𝕭.𝕃. 4⁰.
„ 8⁰.
Burgersdicius (Fr.). Institutionum logicarum libri duo. 8⁰.
Cicero. Epistolae.
Common Prayer. F⁰.
„ 8⁰.
D[uport] (J.). Θρηνοθρίαμβος, seu liber Job graeco carmine. 8⁰.
Morton (Tho.). Antidotum. 4⁰.
Peterborough Visitation Articles. 4⁰.
Sternhold (T.). Psalms in metre. 𝕭.𝕃. 4⁰.
„ „ 8⁰.
„ „ Roman Letter. 4⁰.
Συνῳδία sive Musarum Cantabrigiensium concentus. 4⁰.

1638
Bible. F⁰.
„ 4⁰.
Common Prayer. F⁰.
„ 4⁰.
„ 8⁰.
Directions for musters. 4⁰.
Herbert (Geo.). The Temple. Ed. 5. 12⁰.
Isocrates. Orationes et Plutarchus. 8⁰.
Justa Edouardo King... +Obsequies. 4⁰.
Norwich Visitation Articles. 4⁰.
Ovidius. De tristibus. 8⁰.
Panegyricon inaugurale Praetoris Regii. 4⁰.
Psalms in metre. F⁰.
„ 4⁰.
Winterton (R.). Gerhard. Meditations (Ed. 5) +Prayers (Ed. 6). 12⁰.

1639
Bible. 𝕭.𝕃. 4⁰.
Cade (Anthony). Sermon on Conscience. 4⁰.
Cicero de Officiis. 8⁰.
Davenant (Jo.). Expositio Epistolae ad Coloss. F⁰.
„ „ Determinationes...Edd. 2 and 3. F⁰.
Du Praissac (Sieur). Military Discourses. Englished by J. C[ruso]. 8⁰.
„ „ Short method for the easy resolving etc. 8⁰.
Fuller (Tho.). The Historie of the Holie Warre. F⁰.
Gurnay (Edm.). Towards the vindication of the Second Commandment. 24⁰.
H[odgson] (W.). The Holy Sinner. 12⁰.
Psalms in metre. 𝕭.𝕃. 4⁰.

11—2

1640

Almanacks (Rivers, Swallow). 8⁰.
Ball (J.). A friendly trial of the grounds tending to Separation. 4⁰.
B[enlowes?] (E.). A Buckler against the fear of death. 8⁰.
Bible. 𝕭. 𝕷. 4⁰. (N.T. title 1639.)
Common Prayer. 𝕭. 𝕷. 4⁰
Davenant (J.). Ad fraternam communionem adhortatio. 12⁰.
Downame (G.). A Godly and learned treatise of Prayer. 4⁰.
Drexelius (H.). The School of Patience. 12⁰.
Endeavour (An) of making the principles of the Christian religion plain. 8⁰.
Eustachius (Fr.). Summa philosophiae quadripartita. 8⁰.
Fenner (W.). The Souls Looking-glasse. 8⁰.
Fletcher (Giles). Christs Victory. 4⁰.
Fuller (Tho.). Historie of the Holy Warre. Ed. 2. F⁰.
Gerhard (Joh.). The Summe of Christian Doctrine. 24⁰.
Gower (J.). Ovids Festivalls. 8⁰.
Heinsius (Dan.). Sacrarum exercitationum libri xx. 4⁰.
H[odgson] (W.). The Divine Cosmographer. 12⁰.
[Lily (W.).] A short introduction of grammar. 8⁰.
Morton (Tho.). Decisio controversiae de eucharistia. 4⁰.
Posselius (Joh.). Syntaxis graeca. 8⁰.
Ramus (P.). Dialecticae libri duo. 12⁰.
Randolph (T.). The Jealous Lovers. 8⁰.
Rohan (Henri de). The Complete Captain: trs. by John Cruso. 8⁰.
Voces votivae. 4⁰.
Winterton (R.). Gerhard. Meditations (Ed. 6) + Prayers (Ed. 7). 12⁰.

1641

Andrewes (Lancelot). Nineteen sermons concerning Prayer. 12⁰.
Christian's Pattern, The. 12⁰.
Davenant (John). Animadversions upon a treatise (of S. Hoard). 8⁰.
Dury (J.). On Peace ecclesiastical. 4⁰.
Gataker (T.). Defence of Anthony Wotton. 8⁰.
Herbert (G.). The Temple. Ed. 6. 12⁰.
Heywood (T.). England's Elisabeth. 12⁰.
Irenodia Cantabrigiensis. 4⁰.
Layer (John). Office and Duty of Constables. 8⁰.
L'Estrange (Hamon). Gods Sabbath etc. 4⁰.
Maisterson (Henr.). Sermon on Hebr. xiii. 18. 4⁰.
Manuell, A, or a Justice of Peace his Vade-mecum. 12⁰.
Munning (Humphry). A Pious Sermon etc. 4⁰.
Salernitanus, B. De Fontibus Artium. 12⁰.
Sherman (J.). A Greek in the Temple. 4⁰.
Sternhold (T.). Psalms in metre. 12⁰.
Thorndike (H.). Of the Government of Churches, a Discourse etc. 8⁰.
Warme Beere, or, A Treatise. 12⁰.

1642

Almanacks (Dove, Swallow). 8⁰.
Demosthenes. Orationes Selectae. Gr. et Lat. 12⁰.
Du Praissac (Sieur). Military Discourses. Englished by J. C[ruso]. 8⁰.
Fern (Henry). Resolving of Conscience. 4⁰. (Two states.)

CAMBRIDGE BOOKS 165

Fuller (Tho.). The Holy State [and the Profane State]. F⁰.
His Majesty's Declaration to all His loving Subjects. Aug. 12, 1642. 4⁰.
  ,, Answer to Declaration of Parliament of July 1. 4⁰.
Holdsworth (Ri.). Sermon in St Maries upon Mar. 27. 4⁰.
Kempis of the following of Christ. 8⁰.
Love (Ri.). The Watchman's Watchword. 4⁰.
Magirus (Jo.). Physiologicae Peripateticae libri VI. 8⁰.
More (Hen.). Ψυχωδια Platonica. 8⁰.
Novum Testamentum (Beza). 2 states. F⁰.
Petition of the Commons of Kent. 4⁰.
Petition of Lords and Commons, and His Majestie's Answer. 4⁰.
Proclamation. That no Popish Recusant shall serve. 4⁰.
[Spelman (Sir H.).] A Protestant's Account of his Orthodox Holding. 4⁰.
Thorndike (Herbert). Of Religious Assemblies. 8⁰.
Torriano (G.). Select Italian Proverbs. 12⁰.
Watson (Ri.). Sermon touching Schisme. 4⁰.

1643
Beda. Historia Ecclesiastica. F⁰.
Catalogue of remarkable mercies conferred upon the seven counties. 4⁰.
Fenner (W.). The Souls Looking-Glasse. 8⁰.
Introductio ad Sapientiam. 24⁰.
Jackson (Art.). Help. 4⁰.
Minucius Felix (M.). Octavius. 16⁰.
Quarles (Fra.). Emblemes. Ed. 2. 8⁰.
Revindication of Psalme 105. 5, Touch not mine Anointed. 4⁰.
Swan (John). Speculum Mundi. Ed. 2. 4⁰.

1644
Beda. Historia Ecclesiastica. F⁰.
Burgersdicius (Fra.). Institutionum Logicarum libri II. 8⁰.
Crofts (J.). The Copy of a letter. 4⁰.
Dering (Sir Edw.). A Discourse of Proper Sacrifice. 4⁰.
  ,, ,, A Discourse etc. 4⁰ with different title.
Grimston (Sir H.). A Christian New Years gift. 16⁰.
Lambarde, W. 'Αρχαιονομία. F⁰.
Military Instructions for the Cavallrie. F⁰ (see Cruso 1632).
Swan (J.). Speculum Mundi. 4⁰.
Totius Rhetoricae adumbratio in usum Paulinae Schol. 8⁰.
Winterton (R.). Gerhard. Meditations and Prayers. 12⁰.

1645
Bible. 12⁰. (*N.T. title* 1646.)
Bythner (Victorinus). Lingua Eruditorum. 8⁰.
Chronometra aliquot memorabilium rerum his certis annis gestarum etc. 4⁰.
Crofts (J.). The copy of a letter. Ed. 2. 4⁰.
Howell (James). Δενδρολογία. Dodona's Grove or the Vocal Forest. 12⁰.
Psalms in metre. 4⁰.
Sarson (L.). Analysis of 1 Tim. i. 15; Chronologia Vapulans. 4⁰.
Shelton (T.). Tachygraphy. 8⁰.
Stahl (D.). Axiomata Philosophica. 12⁰.
Torriano (G.). Directions for the Italian Tongue. 4⁰ (n. d.).

1646

Ames (W.). Philosophemata. 12⁰.
Bible. 8⁰.
Britannicus his blessing (in verse). 4⁰.
Buxtorf (Jo.). Epitome Grammaticae Hebraeae. 8⁰.
Duport (J.). Tres libri Solomonis Graeco carmine. 8⁰.
Hall (John). Poems. 8⁰.
Heinsius (Daniel). Crepundia Siliana. 12⁰.
Jackson (Art.). Annotations. 4⁰.
More (Henry). Democritus Platonissans. 8⁰.
Quarles (F.). Judgment and Mercy for afflicted souls. 8⁰.
Sleidan (J.). De quatuor summis Imperiis libri tres. 24⁰.
Sternhold (T.). Psalms. 12⁰.
Valdesso (John). Divine Considerations. 8⁰.

1647

Animadversions upon proceedings against the XI members. 4⁰.
Bible. 12⁰.
Bolton (Sam.). Fast Sermon. 4⁰.
Burgersdicius (F.). Institutiones Logicae. 8⁰.
Cudworth (R.). Sermon before the House of Commons. 4⁰.
Declaration from Sir Thomas Fairfax and his Councell of Warre. 4⁰.
Fuller (Tho.). Historie of the Holie Warre. Ed. 3. F⁰.
Graecae Grammatices compendium...Westm. 8⁰.
Hammond (H.). Five propositions to the Kings Majesty. 4⁰.
H[austed] (P.). πρόσσω καὶ ὀπίσσω. A Sermon at St Maries, 1640. 4⁰.
Heads of a Charge delivered in the name of the Armie.
Introductio ad Sapientiam. 24⁰.
J. (H.). Modell of a Christian Society + Right hand of Christian love. 8⁰.
Letter from the Court at Oatelands. 4⁰.
Manifesto from Sir T. Fairfax June 27. 4⁰.
More (Henry). Philosophicall Poems. Ed. 2. 8⁰.
Papers of Intelligence from Cambridge. 4⁰.
Proclamation by his Excellency Sir Thomas Fairfax. 4⁰.
Representation from Sir Tho. Fairfax. 4⁰.
Shelton (T.). Tachygraphy. 8⁰.
Short introduction to Grammar...Westminster. 8⁰.
Solemn Ingagement. 4⁰.
Stierius (Joh.). Praecepta doctrinae tabellis compacta. Ed. noua. 4⁰.
The Kings majesties declaration and profession.
Two petitions of the Counties of Buckingham and Hertford. 4⁰.
[Vigerius (Fra.).] De praecipuis Gr. dictionis idiotismis. 8⁰.

1648

Anacreon. Odae, Gr. Lat. (ab H. Stephano). 8⁰.
Beaumont (Jos.). Psyche. F⁰.
Bible. 12⁰. (6 eds.)
Bythner (Victorinus). Clavis Linguae Sanctae. 8⁰.
Catechisms (Greek). 12⁰.
Caussin (N.). Christian Diary. 12⁰.
Eustachius (Fr.). Summa Philosophiae Quadripartita. 8⁰.
Fuller (Tho.). Holy and Profane State. Ed. 2. F⁰.

Hill (Tho.). The best and worst of Paul. 4⁰.
Homerus. Ilias. Gr. et Lat. 8⁰.
New Testament. 12⁰.
Wendelin (M. F.). Admiranda Nili. 4⁰.
      „   Contemplationes Physicae. 4⁰.
White (Thos.). The smoak of the botomlesse pit. 8⁰.
Wollebius (J.). Compendium Theologiae Christianae. 12⁰.

1649

Dickson (D.). A Short Explanation of the Ep. of Paul to the Hebrews. 8⁰.
Eustachius. Summa philosophica quadripartita. 8⁰.
Harvey (Wm.). Exercitatio Anatomica de Circulatione Sanguinis. 12⁰.
Jacchaeus (Gilb.). Summa Philosophiae. 12⁰.
Mede (Jos.). Clavis Apocalyptica ex innatis. 4⁰.
Thorndike (H.). Of the Right of the Church in a Christian State. 8⁰.
Torriano (G.). Select Italian Proverbs. 24⁰.

1650

Burgersdijck (Fra.). Collegium Physicum. Editio tertia. 12⁰.
Davenant (John). Dissertationes duae. F⁰.
Pemble (W.). Tractatus de origine formarum. (n. d.) 12⁰.
Thorndike (Herb.). Two Discourses. 8⁰.
Winterton (R.). Drexelius. Considerations upon Eternity. 24⁰.

1651

Castalio (S.). Dialogorum Sacrorum Libri III. 8⁰.
Coldwell. Regulae morum. F⁰.
Culverwell (N.). Spiritual Opticks.
Dillingham (W.). Sir H. Vere, Commentaries of War. F⁰.
Stephens (T.). Statius. Sylvae. 8⁰.
      „   „   Achilleis. 8⁰.
The Second Lash of Alazonomastix. 8⁰.

1652

Beza (T.). Novum Testamentum. F⁰.
Gataker (T.). Antonini Meditationes. 4⁰.
Mede (J.). Opuscula Latina ad rem Apocalypticam. 4⁰.
Nicols (T.). A Lapidarie. 4⁰.
Winterton (R.). Poetae Minores Graeci. 8⁰.

1653

D[uport] (J.). θρηνοθρίαμβος, sive liber Job Graeco carmine. Ed. 2. 8⁰.
Lily (W.). Brevissima Institutio. 8⁰.
Scattergood (A.). Annotationes in Vetus Testamentum. 8⁰.
Smith (T.). Daillé, Apology for the Reformed Churches. 8⁰.

1654

Cambridge Victuallers License (Single leaf).
Dove. Prognostication. 8⁰.
Eustachius. St Paulo: Ethica. 8⁰.
Jacchaeus (T.). Onomasticon Poeticum. 8⁰.
Muretus (H. A.). Terentius. 8⁰.

Oliva Pacis ad Oliverum. 4º.
Smetius. Prosodia. 12º.
Winterton (R.). Drexelius, Considerations upon Eternitie. 12º.

1655
Barrow (I.). Euclid. 8º.
Epictetus. Enchiridion. 8º.
Fuller (T.). History of the University of Cambridge. Fº.
Lucas Holstenius. Porphyrius de Abstinentia. 8º.
Officium Concionatoris. 4º.

1656
Aesopus. Fabulae. 8º.
Dillingham (W.). Two Sermons. 4º.
[„   ] Confessio fidei. 8º.
Muretus (M. A.). Terentius. 8º.

1657
Arrowsmith (J.). Tactica Sacra. 4º.
Bible. 8º.
    „   (N.T. title 1661.)
Corderius (M.). Colloquia. 8º.
Dillingham (W.). Sir F. Vere's Commentaries. Fº.
Dorislaus (I.). Proelium Nuportanum. Fº.
Frost (J.). Select Sermons. Fº.
New Testament. 8º.
Stephanus (H.). Statius, Opera. 8º.
Sternhold (T.). Psalms. 2 eds. 8º.

1658
Aesopus. Fabulae. 8º.
Atwell (G.). The faithfull Surveyor. 4º.
Bible. 16º.
Corderius (M.). Colloquia. 8º.
Frost (J.). Select Sermons. Fº.
Lightfoot (J.). Horae Hebraicae in Chorographiam. 4º.
    „   „   in Evang. Matth. 4º.
Musarum Cantabrigiensium Luctus and Gratulatio. 2 eds. 4º.
Spencer (W.). Origenis contra Celsum. 4º.

1659
Arrowsmith (J.). Armilla Catechetica. 4º.
Aylesbury (T.). Diatribae de aeterno decreto. 4º.
Bible. Fº.
Cicero. De Officiis, de Amicitia, de Senectute. 8º.
[Dillingham (W.).] Confessio Fidei in Latinum versa. 8º.
Ivory (J.). A Continuation.
New Testament. Fº.
University Queries. 4º.

1660
Academiae Cantabrigiensis ΣΩΣΤΡΑ. 2 eds. 4º.
Bible. (N.T. title 1659.) Fº.
Burgersdicius (F.). Institutionum Logicarum Libri duo. 8º

Cicero de Officiis, de Amicitia etc. 8⁰.
Common Prayer. F⁰.
Dunconus (E.). De Adoratione Dei versus Altare. 12⁰.
Duport (J.). Evangelicall Politie. 4⁰.
„ Homeri Gnomologia. 4⁰.
Gardiner (S.). De efficacia gratiae convertentis. 4⁰.
H[acon] (J.). A Review of Mr Horn's Catechisme. 8⁰.
Love (R.). Oratio post regem reducem. 2 eds. 4⁰.
[Ray (J.).] Catalogus plantarum circa Cantabrigiam nascentium. 8⁰.
Smith (T.). The Life and Death of Mr William Moore. 8⁰.
Spencer (J.). The Righteous Ruler. 4⁰.

1661
Almanacks (Pond, Swan). 8⁰.
Bible. 8⁰.
Colet (J.). A Sermon of Conforming and Reforming. 8⁰.
Lily (W.). Short Introduction of Grammar. 8⁰.
New Testament. 8⁰.
Nye (P.). An exact concordance to the Bible.
Poetae Minores Graeci. 8⁰.
Psalms. 8⁰.
Savonarola (H.). The Truth of the Christian Faith. ·12⁰.
Stephens (T.). Three Sermons. 12⁰.
Sternhold (T.). The Whole Book of Psalms. 8⁰.
Threni Cantabrigienses in funere Henrici et Mariae. 4⁰.

1662
Anticlassicus (P.). Vindication of the Inner Temple. 8⁰
Atwell (G.). The Faithfull Surveyour. 4⁰.
Common Prayer. 8⁰.
Duport (J.). Epithalamia Sacra. 8⁰.
Epithalamia Cantabrigiensia Caroli II et Catharinae. 4⁰.
H[acon] (J.). A Vindication of the Review. 8⁰.
Hyde (E.). The true Catholick's Tenure. 8⁰.
Muretus (M. A.). Terentius. 8⁰.
[Newman (S.).] Concordance. F⁰.
New Testament. 8⁰.
Psalms. 8⁰.

1663
Aesopus. Fabulae.
Almanacks (Dove, Pond, Swan).
Bible. 4⁰.
„ 8⁰. (N.T. title 1662.)
Common Prayer. 4⁰.
Fortrey (S.). England's Interest. 8⁰.
Heerebord (A.). Logica (Ἑρμηνεία) seu Synopseos. 8⁰.
Ichabod. 4⁰.
Le Franc (J.). The Touchstone of Truth.
Lightfoot (J.). Horae Hebraicae. 4⁰.
[Ray (J.).] Appendix ad Catalogum. 8⁰ and 12⁰.
Spencer (J.). A Discourse concerning Prodigies. 4⁰
Sternhold (T.) etc. The Whole Book of Psalms. 4ᶜ.

Vossius (G. J.). Elementa Rhetorica.
Winterton (R.). Epigrammata Therapeutica. 8⁰.

1664
Almanacks (Dove, Pond, Swallow, Swan).
Bible. 12⁰.
Homerus. Ilias. 8⁰.
    „   Odyssea. 8⁰.
Psalms (Greek). 12⁰ and 8⁰.
Salmasius (C.). L. Annaeus Florus.
Whear (D.). Methodus legendi historias. 8⁰.

1665
Almanacks (Dove, Pond, Swallow, Swan). 8⁰.
Beaumont (J.). Observations upon the Apologie of Dr Henry More. 4⁰
Bellum Belgicum Secundum. 4⁰.
Castalio (S.). Biblia Sacra.
Common Prayer (Greek). 12⁰ and 8⁰.
Duhamel (J. B.). Elementa Astronomica. 12⁰.
Edwards (J.). The Plague of the Heart. 4⁰.
Fournier (G.). Euclid. 12⁰.
Hoole (C.). Terminations of Declensions. 8⁰.
New Testament (Greek). 2 eds. 12⁰.
Old Testament (Greek). (2 states.) 12⁰.
Sallustius. 12⁰.
Sophocles. Tragoediae. 8⁰.
Swan (J.). Speculum Mundi. Ed. 3. 4⁰.

1666
Almanacks (Dove, Pond, Swallow, Swan). 8⁰.
Bible. 4⁰.
Burgersdicius (F.). Institutionum Logicarum Libri duo. 8⁰.
    „   „   „   Synopsis. 8⁰.
Common Prayer. 4⁰.
Concordance.
Drexelius. Considerations upon Eternitie. 12⁰.
Duport (J.). Psalms in Greek verse. 4⁰.
Heereboord (A.). Ἑρμηνεία Logica. Ed. 2. 8⁰.
New Testament. 4⁰.
Pachymerius (G.). Epitome Logices Aristotelis. 8⁰.
Sternhold (T.). The Whole Book of Psalms. 4⁰.

1667
Almanacks (Dove, Pond, Swan). 8⁰.
[Bullokar (John).] An English Expositour. 12⁰.
Dillingham (T.). Visitation Articles. 4⁰.
Salmasius (C.). Annaeus Florus. 12⁰.
Winterton (R.). Poetae Minores Graeci. 8⁰.

1668
Almanacks (Dove, Pond, Swallow). 8⁰.
Bible. 4⁰.

Bible. (N.T. title 1666.) 4⁰.
Galtruchius (P.). Mathematicae totius Institutio. 8⁰.
Hill (J.). Schrevelius, Lexicon. 4⁰.
Jackson (J.). Index Biblicus. 4⁰.
Kemp (E.). University Sermon. 4⁰.
Sophocles. Scholia. 8⁰.
Starkey (W.). The divine obligation of human ordinances. 4⁰.

1669
Aesopus. Fabulae. 8⁰.
Almanacks (Dove, Pond, Swan, Whiting). 8⁰.
Casaubon (M.). Letter to P. du Moulin. 4⁰.
Dictionarium etymologicum. 4⁰.
Ellis (J.). Clavis Fidei. 8⁰.
Gouldman (F.). Dictionary. Ed. 2. 4⁰.
Heereboord (A.). Logica. 8⁰.
Livius. 8⁰.
Protestant Almanack. 8⁰.
Scargill (D.). Recantation. 4⁰.
Sophocles. Tragoediae. 8⁰.
Spencer (J.). Dissertatio de Urim et Thummim. 8⁰.
Threni Cantabrigienses in exequiis Henriettae Mariae. 4⁰.

1670
Almanacks (Dove, Pond, Swallow, Swan). 8⁰.
Barne (M.). Sermon at Newmarket. 4⁰.
Bible. 4⁰.
Cato. Disticha de moribus cum Scholiis Erasmi. 8⁰.
Common Prayer. 4⁰.
Crashaw (R.). Poemata et Epigrammata. Ed. 2. 8⁰.
„ Steps to the Temple. 8⁰.
Culmann (L.). Sententiae Pueriles. 8⁰.
Dillingham (T.). Visitation Articles. 4⁰.
Gallus (E.). Pueriles Confabulatiunculae. 8⁰.
Hume (J.). Character of a heavenly conversation.
Johnson (J.). The Judges Authority. 4⁰.
„ Nature inverted. 4⁰.
Lacrymae Cantabrigienses in obitum...Henriettae. 4⁰.
Molinaeus (P.). Poematum libelli tres. 8⁰.
New Testament. 4⁰.
Ovid. Tristia. 8⁰.
R[ay] (J.). Collection of Proverbs. 8⁰.
Seignior (G.). Sermon at Saxham. 4⁰.
Sheringham (R.). De Anglorum gentis origine. 8⁰.
Spencer (J.). Dissertatio de Urim et Thummim. Ed. 2. 8⁰.
Sternhold (T.) and others. The Whole Book of Psalms. 4⁰.
Sturm (J.). Cicero, Epistolarum Libri IV. 8⁰.
Threnodia in obitum Georgii Ducis Albaemarlae. 4⁰.
Winterton (R.). Gerhard. Meditations. 12⁰.

1671
Almanacks (Dove, Pond, Swallow, Swan). 8⁰.
B[ullokar] (J.). An English Expositour. 12⁰.

Drexelius. Considerations. 12⁰.
Epicedia in obitum Principis Annae. 4⁰.
Gale (T.). Opuscula Mythologica. 8⁰.
Laney (B.). Ely Visitation Articles. 4⁰.
Lily (W.). Short Introduction of Grammar. 8⁰.
North (J.). Sermon before King at Newmarket. (2 eds.) 4⁰.
Winterton (R.). Poetae Minores Graeci. 8⁰.

1672

Almanacks (Dove, Pond, Swallow, Swan). 8⁰.
Foundation of the University. Broadsheet.
Homer, Iliad.
N[ewman] (S.). Concordance. Ed. 2. F⁰.
Ovid. Metamorphoses. 8⁰.
Pearson (J.). Vindiciae Epistolarum Ignatii (with Vossius, Epistolae). 4⁰.
Puffendorf (S.). Elementa Jurisprudentiae. 8⁰.
Ramus (P.). Dialectic. 8⁰.
Ravisius (J.). Epistolae. 8⁰.
Schrevelius (C.). Hesiod. 8⁰.
Sophocles (Greek and Latin). 8⁰.
Varenius (B.). Geographia Generalis. Ed. I. Newton. 8⁰.

1673

Almanack. 8⁰.
Barclay (J.). Argenis (engraved title 1674). 8⁰.
Bible. 4⁰.
Catechesis in usum scholae Buriensis. 8⁰.
Common Prayer. 4⁰.
Fortrey (S.). England's Interest. Ed. 2. 8⁰.
Friendly Vindication of Dryden. 4⁰.
Grotius. De principiis juris naturalis. 8⁰.
Lily (W.). Short Introduction of Grammar. 8⁰.
North (J.). Plato, Dialogi Selecti. 8⁰.
Smith (J.). Select Discourses. Ed. 2. 4⁰.
Sophocles, Tragoediae. 8⁰.
Sternhold (T.) and others. The Whole Book of Psalms. 4⁰.
Varenius (B.). Descriptio Japoniae. 8⁰.

1674

Almanack (Dove). 8⁰.
Bible. F⁰.
Casimir (M.). Lyricorum Libri. 24⁰.
Cicero. De officiis, etc. 8⁰.
Crashaw (R.). Poemata et Epigrammata. Ed. 2. 8⁰.
Gouldman (F.). Dictionary. Ed. 3.
Lightfoot (J.). Horae Hebraicae. 4⁰.
Olivier (P.). Dissertationes Academicae. 8⁰.
Ovid. Heroides. 8⁰.

1675

Almanack (Swan). 8⁰.
Bible. 4⁰.
Common Prayer. 4⁰.

Faber (T.). Lucretius. De Rerum Natura. 12⁰.
Ivory (J.). A Continuation. Bds.
Jackson (W.). Of the Rule of Faith. 4⁰.
Magna et antiqua charta Quinque Portuum. 8⁰.
M[arvell] (A.). Plain Dealing. 12⁰.
[Rogers (T.).] Faith professed in the xxxix Articles. 4⁰.

1676

Beza (T.). Novum Testamentum. 12⁰.
Briggs (W.). Opthalmographia. 8⁰.
B[ullokar] (J.). An English Expositour. 12⁰.
Common Prayer. 4⁰.
D[uport (J.).] Musae Subsecivae. 8⁰.
Muretus (M. A.). Terentius. 8⁰.
North (Sir T.). Plutarch's Lives. F⁰.
Rhodokanakis (C.). Tractatus de resolutione verborum. 8⁰.
Robertson (W.). Thesaurus Graecae Linguae. 4⁰.
Scattergood (S.). Sermon before king at Newmarket. 4⁰.
Simon (M.). Opera Theologica.
Templer (J.). Visitation Sermon. 4⁰.

1677

Beza (T.). Novum Testamentum. 32⁰.
Bible. 4⁰.
   „   (N.T. title 1675.)
Epithalamium in nuptiis Gulielmi-Henrici Arausii et Mariae. 4⁰.
Spencer (W.). Origen, Contra Celsum. 4⁰.
W[alker] (W.). Plea for Infant Baptism. 8⁰.
Winterton (R.). Poetae Minores Graeci. 8⁰.
Wittie (R.). Gout Raptures. 4⁰.

1678

Almanacks (Dove, Pond, Swallow, Swan). 8⁰.
Babington (H.). Mercy and Judgment. 4⁰.
Badius (J.). Baptista Mantuanus. 8⁰.
Gouldman (F.). Dictionary. Ed. 4. 4⁰.
Ray (J.). English Proverbs. Ed. 2. 8⁰.

1679

Almanacks (Dove, Pond, Swallow, Swan). 8⁰.
Bible. 4⁰.
Common Prayer. 4⁰.
Crashaw (R.). Poemata et Epigrammata. 8⁰.
Heinsius (D.). Andronicus Rhodius, Ethicorum Paraphrasis. 8⁰.
Livius. Historia. 8⁰.
Sallustius. 12⁰.
Sternhold (T.). Psalms. 4⁰.

1680

Almanacks (Culpepper, Dove, Pond, Swallow, Swan). 8⁰.
B[ullokar] (J.). An English Expositour. 12⁰.
Burgersdicius (F.). Institutionarum Logicarum libri duo. 8⁰.

Florus, Pontanus, Ampelius. 12º.
Heerebord (A.). Ἑρμηνεία Logica. Ed. nova. 8º.
New Testament. (Engraved table 1683.) 4º.

1681

Almanack (Wing). 8º.
Hill (J.). Schrevelius, Lexicon. 8º.
Lily (W.). Short Introduction of Grammar. 8º.
Robertson (W.). Phraseologia Generalis. 8º.
[Rogers (T.).] Faith professed in the XXXIX Articles. 4º.
Varenius (B.). Geographia Generalis (ed. Sir Isaac Newton). Ed. 2. 8º.

1682

Almanacks (Culpepper, Dove, Pond, Swallow, Swan, Wing).
Barne (M.). Two University Sermons. 4º.
Bible. 4º.
    „   (N.T. title 1680.) 4º.
    „   („   1666.) 4º.
N[ewman] (S.). Concordance. Ed. 3. Fº.
Pindarick Poem to Duke of Albemarle. Fº.
Puffendorf (S.). De officio hominis et civis. 8º.
Schuler (J.). Exercitationes ad principiorum Descartes primam partem. 8º.

1683

Barne (M.). University Sermon (large paper). 4º.
Bible. 4º.
    „   (N.T. title 1680.) 4º.
    „   („   1666.) 4º.
Common Prayer. 4º.
Davenant (J.). De morte Christi. 12º.
Eusebius, etc. Fº.
Hymenaeus Cantabrigiensis. (2 issues.) 4º.
Jewel (J.). Apologia Ecclesiae Anglicanae. 12º.
North (J.). Plato, Dialogi selecti. Ed. 2. 8º.
Robertson (W.). Manipulus Linguae Sanctae et Eruditorum. 4º.
Sternhold (T.) and others. Psalms. 4º.

1684

Barne (M.). Assize Sermon, Hertford. 4º.
Baronius (R.). Metaphysica. 12º.
Beda. Historia Ecclesiastica. Fº.
Bullokar (J.). An English Expositour. Ed. 7. 8º.
Cambridge University Statuta. 8º.
Casimir (M.). Sarbievii Lyricorum libri IV. 24º.
Euripides. Fº.
Naudaeus (G.). Bibliographica politica. 8º.
Stephanus (H.). Anacreon. 12º.
Whear (D.). De ratione et methodo legendi utrasque historias. 8º.
Winterton (R.). Poetae Minores Graeci. 8º.

1685

Academiae Cantabrigiensis Affectus, decedente Carolo II. 4º.
Almanacks (Culpepper, Dove, Fly, Swallow). 8º.

Baron (R.). Metaphysica Generalis. 8°.
Castalio (S.). à Kempis, De Christo imitando. 12°.
Concordance.
Erasmus (D.). Enchiridion Militis Christiani. 12°.
Faber (T.). Longinus.
Gostwyke (W.). Sermon for victory over rebels. 4°.
Gower (H.). Discourse after death of Peter Gunning. 4°.
Hill (J.). Schrevelius, Lexicon. Ed. 6. 8°.
Lactantius. Opera. 8°.
Prayers for use in Trinity College Chapel. 4°.
Ray (J.). Second Appendix ad Catalogum.
Rhodokanakis (C.). De resolutione verborum.
Robertson (W.). Liber Psalmorum (Hebrew). 12°.
Spencer (J.). De legibus Hebraeorum. F°.
Statuta Academiae Cantabrigiensis. 8°.

1686

Almanack (Wing). 8°.
Articles of Enquiry. 4°.
Homer. Iliad. 8°.
Lucretius. 12°.
[(?) Newton (Sir I.).] Tables for renewing College leases. 8°.
Novum Testamentum.
Robertson (W.). Manipulus Linguae Sanctae. 8°.
Schuler (J.). Exercitationes ad primam partem...Philosophiae. 8°.
Sleidan (J.). De Quatuor Monarchiis. 12°.
Tertullianus, Apologeticus; Minucius Felix. 12°.
Thurlin (T.). Necessity of Obedience to Spiritual Government. 4°.
Turner (F.). Letter to Clergy of Ely. 4°.
Wolf (H.). Isocrates, Orationes et Epistolae. 12°.

1687

Almanacks (Fly, Pond). 8°.
Ovid. Metamorphoses. 8°.
Vincentius Lirinensis. Commonitorium. 12°.

1688

Almanacks (Culpepper, Dove, Pond, Wing). 8°.
Barnes (J.). History of Edward III. F°.
Browne (T.). Concio ad Clerum. 4°.
B[ullokar] (J.). An English Expositor. 12°.
Castalio (S.). à Kempis, De Christo imitando. 12°.
Illustrissimi Principis Ducis Cornubiae Genethliacon. 4°.
Musae Cantabrigienses. Wilhelmo et Mariae. 4°.
Sanderson (R.). Casus Conscientiae Novem. 8°.
[Saywell (W.).] The Reformation justified. 4°.
„ The Office of a Chaplain. 4°.
Valla (L.). De linguae Latinae elegantia. 8°.
Widdrington (R.). Δεῖπνον καὶ Ἐπίδειπνον. 12°.

1689

Almanacks (Dove, Pond, Wing). 8°.
Fleetwood (W.). Sermon in King's College Chapel. 4°.

Homer. Iliad. 4º.
Launoius (J.). Epistolae. Fº.
Musae Cantabrigienses. 4º.

1690

Fuller (S.). Canonica successio. 4º.
Hypomnemata didactica. 8º.
Milner (J.). De Nethinim sive Nethinaeis. 4º.

1691

Hanbury (N.). Supplementum analyticum ad aequationes Cartesianas. 4º.
Heyrick (T.). Miscellany Poems. 4º.
       „   Submarine Voyage. 4º.
Power (T.). Paradise Lost 1 (Latin). 4º.
Walker (T.). Divine Hymns. 4º.

1692

Almanacks (Swallow, Wing). 8º.
Anatomy of a Jacobite. 4º.
De Meronvile (P. C.). Cicero. Orationes Selectae (Delphini). 4º.
Edwards (J.). Enquiry into four remarkable texts of the N.T. 4º.
Eusebius, etc. Fº.
Minellius (J.). Terentius, Comoediae. 4º.
Saywell (W.). The necessity of adhering to the Church of England. 4º.

1693

A new dictionary in five alphabets. 4º.
Jeffery (J.). Sermon at Norwich. 4º.
Knatchbull (Sir N.). Annotations upon difficult texts of N.T. 8º.
Robertson (W.). Phraseologia generalis. 8º.
Russell (J.). Sermon. 4º.
Walker (T.). Assize Sermon. 4º.

1694

Almanacks (Pond, Swallow). 8º.
Barnes (J.). Euripides. Fº.
Elis (J.). Articulorum XXXIX Defensio. 12º.
Milner (J.). Defence of Archbishop Usher. 8º.

1695

Almanacks (Dove, Swallow). 8º.
Censorinus. De die natali. 8º.
Concordance. 12º.
Lacrymae Cantabrigienses in obitum Mariae. 4º.
Lily (W.). Short Introduction of Grammar. 8º.
Whitefoot (J.). A discourse on the power of charity. 8º.

1696

Almanacks (Culpepper, Dove, Pond, Wing). 8º.
Aristotle. De Poetica. 8º.
Busteed (M.). Orationes duae funebres. 12º.

1697

Aesop Naturaliz'd. 8⁰.
Prognostication (Fly). 8⁰.

1698

Almanack (Fly). 8⁰.
Hutchinson (F.). Commencement Sermon. 4⁰.
N[ewman] (S.). Concordance. Ed. 4. F⁰.
Nourse (P.). Commencement Sermon. 4⁰.
Ovid. Metamorphoses. 8⁰.
Patrick (J.), Brady, and Tate. Psalms in metre. 8⁰.

1699

Almanacks (Culpepper, Dove, Fly, Pond, Swallow, Wing). 8⁰.
Cicero. Orationes (Delphini). 8⁰.
Edwards (J.). Commencement Sermon. 4⁰.
Leeds (E.). Methodus Graecam Linguam docendi. 8⁰.
Leng (J.). Sermon before the King at Newmarket. 4⁰.
Marsh (R.). Sermon at St Mary's. 4⁰.
Talbot (J.). Horatius. 4⁰.
Warren (Robt.). The Tablet of Cebes. 12⁰.

1700

Almanacks (Dove, Pond). 4⁰.
Bennet (T.). An Answer to the Dissenters' Pleas. Ed. 2. 8⁰.
Blackall (O.). Commencement Sermon. 4⁰.
Dillingham (W.). Vita Laurentii Chadertoni. 8⁰.
Edwards (J.). Contio et Determinatio pro gradu Doctoratus. 12⁰.
Gaskarth (J.). Commencement Sermon. 4⁰.
        ,,   Concio ad Clerum. 4⁰.
Hare (F.). Sermon at St Mary's. 4⁰.
Le Clerc (J.). Physica. 12⁰.
New Testament (Greek). 12⁰.
[? Newton (Sir I.).] Tables for leases. Ed. 2. 8⁰.
Philips (A.). Life of John Williams. 8⁰.
Syntaxis et Prosodia. 8⁰.
Winterton (R.). Poetae Minores Graeci. 8⁰.

1701

Alleyne (J.). Sermon at Loughborough. 4⁰.
Almanacks (Culpepper, Dove, Fly, Pond, Swallow, Wing). 8⁰.
Annesley (W. A.). Catullus, Tibullus, Propertius. 4⁰.
Bennet (T.). Confutation of Popery. Edd. 1 and 2. 8⁰.
        ,,   Answer to the Dissenters' Pleas. Ed. 3. 8⁰.
Cornwall (J.). Sermon at St Mary's. 4⁰.
Kettlewell (J.). Help to worthy communicating. Ed. 4. 8⁰.
Kuster (L.). De Suida Diatribe. 4⁰.
Laughton (J.). Vergilius, Bucolica, Georgica et Aeneis. 4⁰.
Leeds (E.). Veteres poetae citati ad P. Labbei sententiam. 12⁰.
Leng (J.). Terentius. Comoediae. Ed. 2. 12⁰.
Marsden (R.). Concio ad Clerum. 4⁰.
Milner (J.). Animadversions upon Le Clerc's reflexions.
Puffendorf (S.). De Officiis Hominis et Civis. Ed. 6. 8⁰.
Talbot (J.). Horatius. Ed. 2. 12⁰.

R.   12

1702

Almanacks (Culpepper, Dove, Fly, Pond, Swallow, Wing). 8⁰.
Archbishop of Philippolis' Speech.
Beaumont (J.). Psyche. Ed. 2. F⁰.
Bennet (T.). A Discourse of Schism. Edd. 1 and 2. 8⁰.
Curcellaeus (S.). Synopsis Ethices. 8⁰.
Descartes (R.). Ethice, in methodum et compendium. 8⁰.
Gassendus (P.). Institutio Astronomica. Ed. 6. 8⁰.
Laughton (J.). Vergilius, Bucolica, Georgica et Aeneis. Ed. 2. 4⁰.
Patrick (J.), Brady, and Tate. Psalms in Metre. 8⁰.
Stillingfleet (E.). Origines Sacrae. Ed. 7. F⁰.
Verses on the death of the King.
Whiston (W.). Chronology of the Old Testament.
       „   Harmony of the Four Evangelists. 4⁰.

1703

Bennet (T.). Defence of the Discourse of Schism. 8⁰.
       „   Answer to Mr Shepherd's considerations. 8⁰.
Cellarius (C.). Notitia orbis antiqui. 4⁰.
Crispinus (D.). Ovidius de Tristibus. 8⁰.
Davies (J.). Maximus Tyrius. 8⁰.
Grotius de jure Belli et Pacis, Epitome. Ed. 2. 8⁰.
Piers (W.). Euripides, Medea et Phoenissae. 8⁰.
Whiston (W.). Tacquet, Elementa Geometriae. 8⁰.

1704

Bennet (T.). A Discourse of Schism. Ed. 3. 8⁰.
       „   Answer to Mr Shepherd's considerations. Ed. 2. 8⁰.
       „   Defence of the Discourse of Schism. Ed. 2. 8⁰.
Cassianus Bassus. 8⁰.
Le Clerc (J.). Logica. Ed. 4. 12⁰.
Leeds (E.). Lucian. 8⁰.
Leng (J.). Sermon at consecration of St Catharine's Chapel. 4⁰.
Needham (P.). Geoponica. 8⁰.
Savage (J.). Sermon at Welwyn. 4⁰.
       „   Assize Sermon at Hertford. 4⁰.
Sherwill (T.). Sermon on SS. Simon and Jude. Ed. 2. 4⁰.
       „   University Sermon. 4⁰.
Willymot (W.). Peculiar use of certain Latin words. 8⁰.

1705

Barnes (J.). Anacreon. 12⁰.
       „   Anacreon Christianus. 8⁰.
Bennet (T.). Confutation of Quakerism. 8⁰.
Cambridge Poll Book. F⁰.
Cicero. Epistolae Selectae. 8⁰.
Dawes (Sir W.). University Sermon. 4⁰.
Jeffery (J.). Sermon.
Kuster (L.). Suidas. Lexicon. F⁰.
Le Clerc (J.). Physica. Ed. 2. 8⁰.

Ovid. Tristia (Delphini). 8⁰.
St John (P.). Quatuor Orationes. 4⁰.
Stephens. Sermon.
Tixier (J.). Epistolae. 8⁰.
Whiston (W.). Sermon at Trinity Church. 4⁰.
Willymot (W.). Peculiar Use of certain words in Latin Tongue. Ed. 2. 8⁰.
Woolston (T.). Old Apology revived. 8⁰.

1706

Bennet (T.). Confutation of Popery. Ed. 3. 8⁰.
Bouchery (W.). Hymnus Sacer e libro Judicum V. 4⁰.
Cicero. Orationes (Delphini). 8⁰.
Davies (J.). Caesar (Gr. and Lat.). 4⁰.
Dawson (J.). Lexicon to Greek Testament. 8⁰.
Ockley (S.). Introductio ad Linguas Orientales. 8⁰.
Snape (A.). Sermon before the Princess Sophia. 4⁰.
[Tudway (T.).] Anthems used in King's College Chapel. 8⁰.
Whiston (W.). Essay on Revelation of St John. 4⁰.

1707

Alleyne (J.). Sermon at Leicester. Ed. 2. 4⁰.
Almanacks (Dove, Pond, Wing). 8⁰.
[Bennet (T.).] Answer to the Dissenters' Pleas. Ed. 4. 8⁰.
    ,,   Necessity of Baptism. 8⁰.
Bentley (R.). Visitation Articles. 4⁰. (170 .)
Cannon (R.). Sermon before the Queen at Newmarket. 4⁰.
Davies (J.). Minucius Felix. 8⁰.
Horatius cum lectionibus variis. 12⁰.
[Jenkins.] Defensio S. Augustini. 8⁰.
Laughton (R.). Sheet of questions on Newtonian philosophy.
Newton (Sir I.). Arithmetica Universalis [ed. W. W.]. 8⁰.
Snape (A.). Commemoration Sermon in King's College Chapel. 4⁰.
Virgilius ex edit. Emmesiana.
Webb. Table of University Officers.
Whiston (W.). Praelectiones Astronomicae. 8⁰.

1708

Bennet (T.). Joint Use of precompos'd Forms of Prayer. Edd. 1 and 2. 8⁰.
    ,,   Discourse of Schism. Ed. 2. 8⁰.
Christian Manual of Devotions.
Johnson (T.). Sophocles, Antigone et Trachiniae. 8⁰.
Le Clerc (J.). Physica. Ed. 7. 12⁰.
Waller. Sermon at Bishop Stortford.
Whiston (W.). Accomplishment of Scripture Prophecies. 8⁰.
    ,,   New Theory of the Earth. Ed. 2. 8⁰.

1709

Bennet (T.). A Confutation of Quakerism. Ed. 2. 8⁰.
Bentley (R.). Emendationes ad Ciceronis Tusculanas. 8⁰.
Davies (J.). Cicero, Tusculanae Disputationes. 8⁰.
Needham (P.). Hierocles. 8⁰.

Sherwill (T.). Monarchy the best establishment. 4º.
Verses on the death of the Prince.
Walker. Divine Essays.

1710

Hughes (J.). Chrysostom de Sacerdotio. 8º.
Laughton (R.). Philosophical Questions.
N. (J.). Compendium of Trigonometry. 12º.
Wasse (J.). Sallustius. 4º.
Whiston (W.). Praelectiones Physico-Mathematicae. 8º.
   ,,   Tacquet, Elementa Geometriae. Ed. 2. 8º.

1711

Barnes (J.). Homer. 4º.
Bentley (R.). Horatius. 4º.
Brome (E.). Christian Fasting. 8º.
Green (R.). Demonstration of the truth of the Christian Religion. 8º.
Herodotus, Vita Homeri. 4º.
Laughton (R.). Mathematical Lectures.

1712

Davies (J.). Minucius Felix et Commodianus. 8º.
Duport (J.) and Needham (P.). Theophrastus, Characteres. 8º.
Green (R.). Principles of Natural Philosophy. 8º.
Hughes (J.). Chrysostom de Sacerdotio. Ed. 2. 8º.
Ockley (S.). Oratio Inauguralis. 4º.
Peck. Essay on Study.
Quaestio Medica.
Thirlby (S.). Answer to Whiston's 17 Suspicions. 8º.
Varenius (B.). Geographia generalis. 8º.

1713

[Bentley (R.).] Emendationes in Menandri et Philemonis Reliquias. 8º.
   ,,   Epistola de Johanne Malela. Ed. 2. 8º.
Bentley (T.). Notes on Bentley's Horace. 8º.
Drake (S.). Castilionis de Curiali sive Aulico. 8º.
Jesus College Statutes.
Massey (E.). Plato, de Republica. 8º.
Newton (Sir I.). Principia Mathematica. Ed. 2. 4º.
Oldham (G.). Sermon at Bishop's Stortford. 4º.
Pycroft (S.). Enquiry into Freethinking. 8º.
Thirlby (S.). Defense of the Answer to Whiston. 8º.
Verses upon the Peace.
Waterland (D.). Assize Sermon. Edd. 1 and 2. 4º.
Whiston (W.). Reflexions. Ed. 2. 8º.

1714

Acad. Cant. Carmina Funebria et Triumphalia. Fº.
Bachelors' Statutes. 8º.
Potter (E.). Vindication of our Saviour's Divinity. 8º.
Pycroft (S.). Reflections on the Nature of Contentment. 8º.
Quaestiones una cum carminibus. 8º.

Statutes of the University. 8º.
Varenius (B.). Geographia. 8º.
Waller (J.). University Sermon. 4º.

1715

Acts of Parliament.
Aspinwall (E.). Preservative against Popery. 8º.
Bentley (R.). Sermon on Popery. 8º.
Clemens Alexandrinus.
Green. Sermon at Canterbury.
Innocency of Error. Ed. 2.
Puffendorf (S.). De Officio Hominis et Civis. 8º.
[S. (J.).] Herodotus, Clio. 8º.
Sherlock (T.). Sermon (20 Nov. 1715). 4º.
Tydall. Sermon.
Wright. Sermon (5 Nov. 1715).

1716

Browne (Sir T.). Christian Morals. 12º.
Fleetwood (W.). Charge to the Clergy. Edd. 1 and 2. 4º.
Lyng (W.). Sermon at Yarmouth. 4º.
Needham (P.). University Sermon. 8º.
Pearce (Z.). Cicero de Oratore. 8º.
Sturmy (D.). Discourses. 8º.
[Wake (W.).] Archbishop of Canterbury's Letter. 4º.
Waterland (D.). Thanksgiving Sermon. 8º.
Waterland (T.). Sermon on anniversary of King's accession. 8º.

1717

Bentley (R.). Boyle Lectures etc. 8º. (n.d.)
Laughton (R.). Sermon before the King at King's College Chapel. 2 eds. 8º.

1718

Bentley (R.). Boyle Lectures. 8º. (n.d.)
Bentley (T.). Cicero de Finibus, Paradoxa. 8º.
Colbatch (J.). Commemoration Sermon in Trinity College Chapel. 8º.
Crossinge (R.). Sermon (Peace and Joy). 8º.
Davies (J.). Cicero de Natura Deorum. 8º.
 „ Cicero de Finibus. 8º.
 „ Lactantius. Epitome. 8º.
Whitfield (J.). Assize Sermon at Ely. 8º.
Wotton (H.). Clemens Romanus. 8º.

1719

Booth. Friendly Advice to Anabaptists.
Elegiae Tristes ad pudicitiam exhortantes. 8º.
Needham (P.). Hierocles. 8º.
Plaifere (J.) and others. Tracts concerning Predestination. 8º.
Waterland (D.). A vindication of Christ's divinity. Edd. 1 and 2. 8º.

1720

Cambridge Concordance. Fº.
Descartes (R.). Ethice. 8º.

[*Gastrell (F.).*] *Bishop of Chester's Case.*
Reading (W.). Valesius, Eusebius, etc. Fº.
Waterland (D.). An answer to Dr Whitby's reply. 8º.
„   Eight sermons. Edd. 1 and 2. 8º.
„   Vindication of Christ's divinity. Ed. 3. 8º.

1721

Barnes (J.). Anacreon. Ed. 2. 12º.
Davies (J.). Cicero, De Divinatione. 8º.
Maichelius (D.). Introductio ad Historiam Literariam. 8º.
Waterland (D.). Arian Subscription. Edd. 1 and 2. 8º.
„   Vindication of Christ's divinity. Ed. 4. 8º.
„   Sermon at St Paul's. 8º.

1722

Cotes (R.). Harmonia Mensurarum. 4º.
Covel (J.). Account of Greek Church. Fº.
Davies (J.). Cicero, De officiis. 8º.
Jortin (J.). Lusus Poetici. 4º.
King (J.). Epistola ad J. Friend. 8º.
Smith (J.). Beda, Historia Ecclesiastica. Fº.
Waterland (D.). Supplement to Arian Subscription. 8º.
Whiston (W.). Tacquet, Elementa Geometriae. Ed. 3. 8º.
Whitfield (J.). Visitation Sermon at Ely. 8º.

1723

Davies (J.). Cicero, Tusculanae Disputationes. Ed. 2. 8º.
„   De Natura Deorum. Ed. 2. 8º.
Hare (F.). Cicero (Manutii).
Leng (J.). Terentius. Ed. 3. 12º.
Markland (J.). Epistola critica ad F. Hare. 8º.
Middleton (C.). Bibliothecae Cantabrigiensis Ordinandae Methodus. 4º.
Piers (W.). Euripides, Medea et Phoenissae. Ed. 2. 8º.
Short Introduction to Grammar, for the use of Bury School.

1724

Bentley (R.). Boyle Lecture Sermons. Ed. 5. 8º.
Doughty (G.). Sermon in King's College Chapel. Edd. 1 and 2. 4º.
Drake (S.). Concio ad Clerum. 4º.
[Gooch.] Caius College Statutes. 8º.
Harding (C.). Vida, Poetica.
Hennebert (C.). Terence in French and Latin.
Newcome (J.). University Sermon. Edd. 1 and 2. 4º.
Parne (T.). Sermon at Bedford. 4º.
Rolfe (T.). Syllabus of Anatomy.
Shuckford (S.). Sermon at Norwich. 4º.
Waterland (D.). Critical History of Athanasian Creed. 8º.
Whitfield (J.). Sermon at St Mary's. 8º.

1725

Bentley (R.). Remarks upon a late Discourse of Free-Thinking. Ed. 6. 8º.
Davies (J.). Cicero, Academica. 8º.
Dawson (J.). Lexicon to Greek Testament. Ed. 2. 8º.

Harris (S.). Oratio Inauguralis. 4º.
Poll for Knights of the Shire of the County of Cambridge.
Whitfield (J.). University Sermon. 8º.

1726

Arnald (R.). Sermon at Bishop Stortford. 4º.
Bentley (R.). Terentius, Phaedrus, Publilius Syrus. 4º.
Davies (J.). Curae Secundae in Caesaris Commentarios. 8º.
King (J.). Euripides, Hecuba, Orestes, Phoenissae. 8º.
Knight (S.). Life of Erasmus. 8º.
Paris (J.). Miscellanea Practico-Theoretica. 8º.

1727

Academiae Luctus in Obitum Georgii I. Fº.
Chappelow (L.). Spencer, De legibus Hebraorum. Fº.
Davies (J.). Cicero, De legibus. 8º.
„ Caesar, Opera. 8º.
Green (R.). Expansive and Contractive Forces. Fº.
Inglis (A.). Bentivoglio's Lettres in Italian. 8º.
Stebbing (H.). Polemical Tracts. Fº.

1728

Aristotle, Poetica (Ed. Goulstoniana 2).
Battie (W.). Aristotelis Rhetorica. 8º.
Blomfield (B.). University Sermon. 8º.
Davies (J.). Cicero, De finibus. 8º.
Edwards. Poem on Copernican System.
Hough (T.). Sermon at St Paul's School. 4º.
Long (R.). Commencement Sermon. Edd. 1 and 2. 4º.
[Newcome (S.).] Enquiry into evidence of Christian Religion. 8º.
Objections against Book of Daniel considered.
Waterland (D.). Critical History of Athanasian Creed. Ed. 2. 8º.

1729

Baker (W.). Sermon preached at Lichfield. 4º.
Battie (W.). Isocrates. 8º.
Cicero, Orationes (Delphini). 8º.
Disney (J.). View of Ancient Laws against Immorality. Fº.
Knight (S.). Spittall Sermon at St Bridget's. 4º.
Stebbing (H.). Defence of Confirmation. 4º.
Warren (M.). Epistle on Abuse of Bark in Fevers. 4º.

1730

Davies (J.). Cicero de Divinatione. Ed. 2. 8º.
„ „ Tusculanae. Ed. 3. 8º.
„ „ *Philosophica.* 8º.
Kent (N.). Excerpta ex Luciani operibus. 8º
Quaestiones una cum carminibus. 8º.
[Waterland (D.).] Advice to a young student. Ed. 2. 8º.

1731

[Chapman (J.).] Remarks on a letter to Dr Waterland. 8º.
[Gretton (P.).] Concio ad Clerum. 8º.

Johnson (T.). On Moral Obligation. 8⁰.
    ,,   University Sermon. 8⁰.
Law (E.). King's Origin of Evil. 4⁰.
Mounteney (R.). Demosthenes, Selectae orationes. 8⁰.
Trevigar (L.). Conic Sections. 4⁰.
[Waterland (D.).] Scripture Vindicated. Pt. II. 8⁰.
Welchman (E.). Tertullianus de Trinitate Liber. 8⁰.

1732

[Chapman (J.).] Remarks on Christianity as old as Creation. 8⁰.
Common Prayer. 8⁰.
Cotes (R.). Harmonia Mensurarum. 4⁰.
Crossinge (S.). Sermon before King William at Newmarket. 2 eds. 4⁰.
Davies (J.). Cicero de Natura Deorum. 8⁰.
Gretton (P.). Conciones duae. 8⁰.
[Johnson (T.).] Quaestiones Philosophicae. 12⁰.
Pearce (Z.). Cicero, De Oratore. Ed. 2. 8⁰.
University Statutes. 8⁰.

1733

Chapman (J.). Remarks on Christianity as old as Creation. 8⁰.
Colbatch (J.). Marriage-treaty between Charles II and Catherine. 4⁰.
Collection of Poems. 8⁰.
Common Prayer. 8⁰.
Davies (J.). Cicero, De Natura Deorum. Ed. 3. 8⁰.
Gratulatio Acad. Cantab. Principis Auriaci nuptias celebrantis. F⁰.
Markland (J.) and Hare (F.). Epistola Critica. 8⁰.

1734

Chapman (J.). Examination of Sykes on Phlegon. 8⁰.
Clarke (Joseph). Further Examination of Dr Clarke on Space. 8⁰.
Clarkson (C.). Visitation Sermon at Melton Mowbray. 4⁰.
Guarini (G. B.). Il Pastor Fido. 4⁰.
Johnson (T.). Letter to Mr Chandler. 8⁰.
Law (E.). Enquiry into the ideas of Space, Time, etc. 8⁰.
Mason (C.). Oratio Woodwardiana. 4⁰.
Rowning (J.). Natural Philosophy. Pt. I. 8⁰.

1735

[? Arbuthnot (J.).] Critical Remarks on Gulliver's Travels. 8⁰.
Bentley (R.). Boyle Lecture Sermons. Ed. 6. 8⁰.
Chapman (J.). Re-examination of Phlegon. 8⁰.
Johnson (T.). Puffendorf de Officiis. 12⁰.
    ,,   Quaestiones Philosophicae. Ed. 2. 12⁰.
Kerrich (S.). Commencement Sermon. 8⁰.
Kynnesman. Latin Grammar. Ed. 2.
Lyons (I.). Hebrew Grammar. 8⁰.
Middleton (C.). Origin of Printing in England. 4⁰.
Pastoral poem on the death of Lord How at Barbados. F⁰.
Rowning (J.). Natural Philosophy, Pt. II. 8⁰.
Waterland (D.). Discourse of Fundamentals. 8⁰.

1736

Davies (J.). Cicero, Academica. Ed. 2. 8º.
Gratulatio Acad. Walliae Principis nuptias celebrantis. Fº.
Pigg (T.). Assize Sermon at Thetford. 4º.
Warren (R.). Answer to Plain Account of Sacrament [by B. Hoadly]. 8º.

1737

Arnald (R.). Sermon at Leicester. 4º.
Bentley (R.). Remarks upon a late Discourse of Free-Thinking. Ed. 7. 8º
Catalogue of Mr Johnson's books.
Muscut (J.). Visitation Sermon at Bedford.
Warren (R.). Appendix to Answer. 8º.
Waterland (D.). Review of Doctrine of Eucharist. 8º.

1738

Catalogue for a sale of books by Thurlbourn.
Davies (J.). Cicero, Disputationes Tusculanae. Ed. 4. 8º.
Lyons (I.). Hebrew Grammar. Ed. 2. 8º.
[Newcome (S.).] Nature and end of the Sacrament. 8º.
Pietas Acad. in funere Principis Wilhelminae Carolinae. Fº.
Smith (R.). Compleat System of Opticks. 4º.
Williams (P.). University Sermon. 4º.

1739

Chapman (J.). Eusebius or the true Christian's Defense. 8º.
[Colbatch (J.).] Treatise for altering the present method of letting leases. 8º.
Cradock (J.). University Sermon. 4º.
Dunthorne (R.). Astronomy of the Moon. 8º.
Law (E.). King, Origin of Evil. Ed. 3. 8º.
Weston (W.). Two Sermons. 8º.

1740

Saunderson (N.). Elements of Algebra. 4º.
Taylor (J.). Lysias. 8º.
    „   Appendix to Suidas.

1741

Chapman (J.). De aetate Ciceronis de legibus. 8º.
Colbatch (J.). The Case of Proxies. 8º.
Davies (J.). Cicero de Finibus. Var. Ed. 2. 8º.
    „   de Divinatione. Ed. 3. 8º.
    „   de Legibus. 8º.
Davies (R.). Memoirs of Dr Nicholas Saunderson. 4º.
Garnett (J.). Assize Sermon. 4º.
Johnson (T.). Quaestiones Philosophicae. Ed. 3. 8º.
Keill (J.). Introductio ad veram Physicam. Ed. 6. 8º.
Squire (S.). Defense of the Antient Greek Chronology. 8º.
[„   ] The Ancient History of the Hebrews. 8º.
Taylor (J.). Demosthenes. Vol. III. 4º.
The Inward Call to the Holy Ministry.
Tunstal (J.). Epistola ad C. Middleton. 8º.

1742

Abridgement of Acts of Parliament relating to Excise. 8⁰.
Catalogue of Duplicates in Royal Library. 8⁰.
Long (R.). Astronomy. Vol. i. 4⁰.
Taylor (J.). Commentarius ad Legem Xviralem. 4⁰.

1743

Bally (G.). Solomon de Mundi Vanitate. 4⁰.
[Bentley (R.).] Remarks on a late discourse of Free-thinking. Ed. 8. 8⁰.
Bible. 12⁰.
Common Prayer. 8⁰.
       ,,   ,,   12⁰.
       ,,   ,,   32⁰.
Law (E.). Assize Sermon, Carlisle. 8⁰.
Newcome (J.). Sermon before the House of Commons. 4⁰.
Richardson ( ). Godwin. De praesulibus Angliae. F⁰.
Rutherforth (T.). Ordo Institutionum Physicarum. 4⁰.
Smart (C.). Carmen Alex. Pope in S. Caeciliam. F⁰.
Taylor (J.). Demosthenes in Midiam et Lycurgus contra Leocratem. 8⁰.
      ,,   Marmor Sandvicense. 4⁰.
Wesley (S.). Poems. Ed. 2. 8⁰.

1744

Butler (S.). Hudibras. 2 vols. 8⁰.
Davies (J.). Cicero de Natura deorum. Ed. 4. 8⁰.
Grey (Z.). Review of Neal's History of the Puritans. 8⁰.
Rutherforth (T.). Nature and obligations of virtue. 4⁰.
Squire (S.). Plutarchus de Iside et Osiride. 8⁰.
Sternhold (T.). The Whole Book of Psalms. 32⁰.

1745

Bennet (P.). University Sermon. 8⁰.
Common Prayer. F⁰.
       ,,   ,,   8⁰.
       ,,   ,,   12⁰.
Davies (J.). Cicero de Legibus. Ed. 2. 8⁰.
Dawes (R.). Miscellanea Critica. 8⁰.
Elstobb (W.). Pernicious consequences of replacing Sluices. 8⁰.
Garnett (J.). Commemoration Sermon. 4⁰.
Law (E.). Considerations on the state of the world. 8⁰.
Tryal of Jeroms and Footman. 8⁰.
Warner (M.). Sermon on the present rebellion. 8⁰.
      ,,   Fast Sermon. 8⁰.
Williams (P.). Sermon at Starston. 8⁰.

1746

[A Divine.] Nature and Necessity of Catechising. 8⁰.
Bateman (W.). Concio ad Clerum. 4⁰.
Bible (Welsh). 8⁰.
Kerrich (S.). Thanksgiving Sermon. 8⁰.
Knowles (T.). The existence and attributes of God. 8⁰.
Mays (C.). Thanksgiving Sermon. 8⁰.

[Powell.] Heads of Lectures in Experimental Philosophy. 8⁰.
Psalms (Welsh). 8⁰.
Rutherforth (T.). Determinatio Quaestionis Theologicae. 4⁰.
      „   Sermon before the House of Commons.
Smart (C.). Carmen Alex. Pope in S. Caeciliam Latine redditum. Ed. 2. 4⁰.
Warner (M.). Thanksgiving Sermon. 8⁰.
Warren (Rich.). Mutual duty of minister and people. 4⁰.
Weston (W.). Rejection of Christian Miracles by Heathens. 8⁰.
      „   Moral impossibility of conquering England. 8⁰.

1747
Bible. 12⁰.
Cotes (R.). Hydrostatical and Pneumatical Lectures. Ed. 2. 8⁰.
Heathcote (R.). Historia Astronomiae. 8⁰.
Taylor (J.). Demosthenes. 8⁰.

1748
Brooke (Z.). Defensio Miraculorum. 4⁰.
Common Prayer. F⁰.
      „   „   12⁰. (2 eds.)
Goodall (H.). Duties attending a proper discharge of the Ministry. 4⁰.
Gratulatio Acad. Cant. de reditu Georgii II. F⁰.
Rutherforth (T.). System of Natural Philosophy. 2 vols. 4⁰.
Sternhold (T.). The Whole Book of Psalms. 12⁰. (2 eds.)
Weston (W.). On the remarkable wonders of antiquity. 8⁰.

1749
Beaumont (J.). Poems. 4⁰.
Bennet (P.). Two University Sermons. 8⁰.
Fauchon (J.). A publick lecture to La Butte. 4⁰.
Green (J.). Commencement Sermon. 4⁰.
Law (E.). Considerations on the state of the world. Ed. 2. 8⁰.
      „   Discourse upon the life of Christ. 8⁰.
Mason [W.]. Installation Ode. 4⁰.
Moody (S.). Concio Academica. 8⁰.
[Ross (J.).] Cicero, Epistolae. 8⁰.
Smith (R.). Harmonics. 8⁰.
Sternhold (T.). The Whole Book of Psalms. 12⁰.
Taylor (J.). Sermon at Bishop-Stortford. 4⁰.

1750
Chapman (T.). On the Roman Senate. 8⁰.
Common Prayer. 12⁰.
[Grey (Z.).] Historical account of Earthquakes. 8⁰.
Hubbard (H.). Sermon at Ipswich. 4⁰.
Knowles (T.). Existence and Attributes of God. 8⁰.
[Masters (R.).]. List of...members of Corpus Christi College. 4⁰.
Michell (J.). Treatise of artificial magnets. 8⁰.
Rutherforth (T.). Defence of [Sherlock's] discourses. Edd. 1 and 2. 8⁰.
Smart (C.). On the Eternity of the Supreme Being. 4⁰.

INDEX